ZÓPHIËL;

OR,

THE BRIDE OF SEVEN.

BY

MARIA DEL OCCIDENTE,

(MARIA GOWEN BROOKS.)

EDITED BY

ZADEL BARNES GUSTAFSON,

AUTHOR OF "MEG, A PASTORAL," AND OTHER POEMS.

BOSTON:
LEE AND SHEPARD, PUBLISHERS.
NEW YORK:
CHARLES T. DILLINGHAM.
1879.

CONTENTS.

MARIA DEL OCCIDENTE.

"My purpose had now become fixed; and, despite of the night I had passed, my appearance, though pale, was *calm to those around me:* but, if the soul which now warms me be eternal, the remembrance of that day, so calm to those around me, will continue to the latest eternity. . . . I next looked over a small trunk of papers. From time to time they have been saved, when my imagination was under the influence of a *strong but vague hope that I should one day or other be loved and renowned, and live longer than my natural life in the history of the country of my forefathers,* and in that where I first beheld the light. Now, I said, no mortal shall smile at the fancies of lonely Idomen."

Idomen; or, The Vale of Yumuri.

IN Cuba, near Limonal, on the San Patricio coffee-estate Cafétal Hermita, stand, now crumbling in picturesque decay, the ruins of a small Grecian temple, where, some thirty years ago, the very passion-flower of womanly genius exhaled itself away. The flight of steps leading to this little temple is overgrown with clambering vines, that mingle their dark leaves and gay flowers across the deserted entrance. The path leading to it is an avenue of stately palms, whose matted leafage completely shelters the way from the sun; while the straight shafts of the palms, wound about with ipomœa and convolvuli, have the appearance of themselves putting forth the rich blossoms of these vines.

The little temple is bowered in a labyrinth of orange-trees, cocoas, and palms, the mango and rose-apple, the ruddy pomegranate and shady tamarind; while the coffee-fields spread away in alternate tessellation of white flowers and scarlet berries.

A traveller thus alludes to this fair retreat: "I have often passed it in the still night, when the moon was shining brightly, and the leaves of the cocoa and palm threw fringe-like shadows on the walls and floor, and the elfin lamps of the cocullos swept through the windows and the door, casting their lurid and mysterious light on every object, while the air was laden with the mingled perfumes of the coffee-wreaths and orange-flowers, the tuberose and night-blooming cereus; and have thought no fitter birthplace could be found for the images she created."

Here, in the retirement of the rarely-disturbed repose and beauty of Hermita, lived and passed away, almost unheard and unnoticed, "Maria del Occidente," one of earth's great singers, whose numbers, having always grace and sweetness, have often also the majesty and the fervid pathos wrung in a narrower tide from Mrs. Caroline Norton by her passionate sense of her own wrongs, and from Mrs. Browning by her yearning compassion over others' woes.

And, to crown these gifts, Maria del Occidente had a pure recognition of the Infinite design as manifested through the mysterious passion of love, which, in its full, simple, unabashed expression, makes her "Zóphiël" among the bravest and the most modest of the creations of genius.

Eighty-two years ago, in the town of Medford, Mass., she was little Maria Gowen, a baby girl, around whom no special hopes were clustered, and whose baby brows foreshadowed neither the glory nor the sorrows of the poet's purple-fruited laurel.

She was born and bred American; but it is not unlikely that the blood of the Welsh bards, from whom she claimed lineage, may have tinctured the fine current of her veins. Her short life of only fifty years was one of comparatively little outward incident: yet these, mostly of her own shaping, indicate the dignity and strength of her character, and mark her stainless wifehood and her devoted motherhood. But her poems, especially her great work "Zóphiël," show that her mental and spiritual life was a passionately vivid æon of intense experiences; and beneath the strong music of her verse breathes ever the cry of the conscious isolation of great gifts, the supreme longing for complete human sympathy.

In all the individual utterances of high desire or passionate feeling throughout "Zóphiël," it is her own soul, imprisoned by fate, yet liberated by genius, that pleads, yet heroically endures. "Zóphiël" was first published entire in London by Kennett, under the care and fostering of Robert Southey, who, in "The Doctor," quotes from the sixth canto of "Zóphiël:" —

"The bard has sung, God never formed a soul
 Without its own peculiar mate, to meet
Its wandering half, when ripe, to crown the whole
 Bright plan of bliss, most heavenly, most complete.

"But thousand evil things there are that hate
 To look on happiness: these hurt, impede,
And, leagued with time, space, circumstance, and fate,
 Keep kindred heart from heart, to pine and pant and bleed.

"And as the dove to far Palmyra flying
 From where her native founts of Antioch beam,
Weary, exhausted, longing, panting, sighing,
 Lights sadly at the desert's bitter stream;

"So many a soul o'er life's drear desert faring —
 Love's pure congenial spring unfound, unquaffed —
Suffers, recoils; then, thirsty and despairing
 Of what it would, descends, and sips the nearest draught."

And adds, "So sings Maria del Occidente, the most impassioned and most imaginative of all poetesses." "The London Quarterly Review," with restricted appreciation, admitted Southey's praise, after substituting the word "fanciful" for "imaginative." Charles Lamb, with that peculiar conceit which we may term the obsolete characteristic of great men, enforced by the potent thrall of "Zóphiël," rose from the reading of it with these words: "Southey says it is by some Yankee woman: as if there had ever been a woman capable of any thing so great!"

With all that can be gleaned from reviews and the brief contemporaneous sketches which followed the publication of this work, and were revived with some slight additions at her death, her life is involved in great obscurity, which I have found it difficult to penetrate, and have been able to disperse only in faint and narrow lines, even after the continued and earnest effort and research of several years.

Her single prose story "Idomen," of which I shall speak later, is undoubtedly autobiographical; and within the limits of that vivid little sketch are the chief clews to the exceptional experiences of her private history. Her father was a gentleman of literary tastes and cultivation, intimate with the Harvard professors. Nowhere do I find any mention of her mother. Rufus Wilmot Griswold, in "The Encyclopedia of American Literature" of 1856, in "The Female Poets" (1853), and in "The Southern Literary Messenger" (1839), gives the most adequate sketch of our author's life. He knew and corresponded with her in her later years; and says, that, when only nine years old, little Maria Gowen's poetic temperament and power were clearly indicated by her avid committal to memory "of passages from 'Comus,' 'Cato,' and the ancient classics." That she became a student of wide and accurate learning is disclosed in her works; the notes of "Zóphiël" alone being a groundwork of erudition, as thickly sprinkled with occult bits of thought, research, and profound study, as the tunic and tresses of an odalisque with gems.

On the death of her father, she was engaged, at the early age of fourteen, to Mr. Brooks, a wealthy Boston merchant, and soon after married to him; and, after reverses of fortune resulting in poverty, she turned her attention to the definite expression of her genius, and at twenty had written a poem in seven cantos, which was never published. In 1820 she issued the little volume, "Judith and Esther, and Other Poems, by a Lover of the Fine Arts," whose genuine poetic worth met with some appreciation. In 1823, becoming a widow, she went to Cuba, making her home with a relative, and there wrote the first canto of "Zóphiël, or The Bride of Seven," publishing it in Boston in 1825. After the death of an uncle, a Cuban planter, whose property, left to her, placed her in easy circumstances as the possessor of a fixed income, she returned to the United States, and lived near Dartmouth College, where her son, Capt. Horace Brooks of the United-States army, was then studying, and where she made studious use of the Dartmouth-College Library. In 1830 she went with a brother to Paris, and in London met Washington Irving, who most kindly encouraged her in the production of her poem. But it was with Southey, at Keswick, where she passed the spring of 1831, that she entered into that strong and sympathetic friendship which fed her pure aspiration with the appreciation and hope that kindle and assure.

Fortunately I can swell these slender outlines with some brief testimony from persons still living, to whom I would here express my grateful acknowledgments.

In 1872, her son, then stationed at Fort M'Henry, Baltimore, Md., wrote to me as follows:—

"I received your note, addressed to the Rev. C. Brooks, Medford, through my cousin Mrs. Ellen Parker of Boston. I have no papers of my mother's near me, nor can I at present get at them. I have, however, a fine miniature done by a young artist (at the time it was taken), which is probably the best likeness that can now be obtained, and which I will forward to you. . . . When I was in Cuba in 1846, the little dilapidated temple (built to gratify my mother by her brother) on the San Patricio coffee-estate, in which most of 'Zóphiël' was written, was still standing; also a monument — a granite base surmounted by a marble cross — at Limonal, not far from Matanzas, erected by me, at mother's request, over my two brothers. There is her resting-place by their side. I cut her name upon the marble with my own hand, to correspond with the inscription which mother placed over her sons."

In July, 1872, I wrote to him, begging him to send me the picture of his mother, and requesting fullest particulars of her life and death, her character and peculiarities, and all details and incidents of interest. To this Col. Brooks replied: —

"FORT M'HENRY.

"The first peculiarity of my mother was that she wrote a round and remarkably plain hand, which I do not, and which you must excuse, for the reason that I seldom write for publication. I will send the miniature. I have but one copy of 'Judith and Esther,' which I fear to part with, as I know not where to get another. My changeable life has prevented my keeping any thing safely. I cannot at present get at any papers of my mother's, and do not know that there are any left such as you might desire.

"The little temple (of which I have no picture, nor of the monument) was built about 1825, and my mother died about 1845. I recollect it when a boy, as a pretty little toy at the end of a beautiful avenue, four rows deep, of palms interspersed with orange-trees and many other tropical plants. It was a charming spot, and illustrates mother's admiration of the picturesque.

"Whatever charm there may be in 'Zóphiël,' and whatever talent it may portray, much undoubtedly is due to the surroundings of the miniature temple where the poem was imagined, and its verse constructed, by a nature as passionate as the name of the flower would indicate which she always wore in her hair, — the only simple adornment of naturally thick and beautiful tresses.

"A lady of position recently visited this fort, and spoke to me of recollecting my mother's peculiarity of dressing always in white, even to white-silk stockings and slippers: *en dame blanche* probably originated in some similar peculiarity. My mother's special characteristic was individuality. She generally succeeded in her endeavors.

"For instance, she applied to have me sent to West Point, and sent me to Washington in 1829 with letters, &c. The appointment was promised, but by some influence was overruled. She then took me to Hanover, N.H., with a view to my entering Dartmouth College. In the mean time she went with her Quebec brother to Europe, where she visited Southey, and by his advice and protection got out a London edition of 'Zóphiël.' She was introduced to Lafayette, who was so pleased with her, that he urged to know if he could be of any service to her. 'Yes,' said she: 'you can get my son into West Point.' Upon this Lafayette wrote to Bernard, our then chief engineer; and the appointment of a cadet came to me.

"Southey was undoubtedly much interested in the American authoress; for when, after his death, I visited his family, they asked for the correspondence as their right, and I subsequently sent several letters to them."

Upon receipt of this letter, with the promised portrait of his mother, I wrote again, thanking him for the use of it, and saying that the completion of this tribute still depended greatly upon him, which I explained as follows: —

"Since my last letter to you I have heard from Richard Hengist Horne of London, who has cordially interested himself to gain information in this matter. He has obtained a hint from Robert Browning, and is in communication with Alfred Tennyson. Mr. Horne is an indefatigable worker, a man of brilliant abilities, with a wide and intimate acquaintance among distinguished men and women. Our own venerable poet Longfellow, during a recent visit at his home in Cambridge, told me that the most important step in my effort to write effectively of your mother was to secure the examination of her private papers. I told him what you had written about their being difficult of access; but he seemed to feel sure you would overcome all difficulties, or put me in the way of doing so. If you cannot obtain the papers yourself, will you not tell me where they are, or authorize me to get them myself? I need hardly assure you that I will take the utmost care of them, and use your confidence with the delicacy due to it and to her memory. I entreat this favor of you in your mother's name, since it is for her sake."

Col. Brooks very kindly sent me his copy of "Judith and Esther," and also of "Idomen," and continued his account: —

"My mother was quite a linguist. She read and wrote fluently in French, Spanish, and Italian; she also sang many songs in these tongues. She was a hard student, and a woman of much research, and very particular to obtain her authority from the original; and often attempted, with the assistance of some friend, the translation of obscure languages. I remember that she kept by her a Persian grammar, and often referred to it. She was also quite an artist, and several pieces painted by her in water-colors were hanging up about her rooms. She had a remarkable memory; and many curious facts she had stored in her mind, in scraps of poetry she had learned in her youth.

"Indeed, her mind took a poetical current from its earliest years. She had a remarkably beautiful form. I have heard her say, that when young, before the days of flowing skirts, when dresses were scant, she often felt ashamed of herself on account of what are now considered curves of beauty being then too well defined. She was a constant attendant at church, and always carried with her an English edition of the services of the church; but she detested all cant and hypocrisy. She was very particular about her own language, disliked all interpolations, and always referred to Johnson and Walker. It was delightful to hear her converse. Her knowledge of present and past events, and of the prominent characters of history, was astonishing. She would tell anecdotes of persons so varied and interesting, that her quiet and unassuming conversation was sought and listened to by many distinguished persons.

"I remember of her travelling with her brother several miles in order to see an Indian chief, and get the precise accent and signification of an Indian word."

In 1874 I wrote again to Col. Brooks, then in Presidio, San Francisco, with reference to his mother's private letters and papers; offering to relieve him from all inconvenience and expense by sending a responsible person for them, if he would consent, and designate their abiding-place. To this he replied substantially as before, that they were scattered about, he hardly knew where himself; that no one but he could "unravel the condition of affairs," and it was impossible for him to come East at present.

In the intervals between this correspondence with the son I met with the most cordial response in other directions of inquiry. In July, 1872, I received the following kind letter from her niece, Mrs. Ellen Parker of Boston:—

"Your letter to the Rev. Mr. Brooks was sent to me, I being a niece of Maria del Occidente; and I thought it the best way to assist you in the beautiful work you think of undertaking to forward your letter to Col. Horace Brooks, her only remaining son, and he, of course, would have in his possession what you would require. In all my life, I never passed more than a few months in the society of my aunt, Mrs. Brooks; but to my girlish vision she always appeared a being of the most romantic loveliness and grace. She *always* dressed in white or gray, wearing transparent sleeves, through which her beautiful arms were seen; and her hands were almost always covered in white-kid gloves. She seemed to *reverence* her own personal charms, and felt it a duty to preserve her own sweetness. When past the meridian of life, her hair and teeth were as beautiful as those of a young girl. I should say that a keen sense of truth and justice, and the most delicate perceptions and actual worship of beauty, were the predominant traits of her character. I regret that I have nothing in my possession which would assist you."

The Rev. Alfred Brooks (brother of the late Rev. Charles Brooks of New-England fame as the "Father of Normal Schools"), to whom I wrote, supposing him to be a relative of the poetess, — in which supposition I was mistaken, — interested himself most kindly to open a way for me; and it is to him I owe the foregoing graceful letter from Mrs. Parker, as well as my first letter from Col. Brooks, and the perusal of one from Miss Lucy Osgood, who, in mentioning a visit of Mrs. Maria Gowen Brooks to Medford, says, "I have a dim recollection of a lady walking out at odd hours, and dressed in white at odd seasons, and of being told that she was Mrs. Brooks, of the Gowen family, a poetess. She and her family soon disappeared; and I afterward found, chiefly through a long respectful article in one of the English reviews, that we had had a flower of genius among us, and in our stupidity knew it not."

By another Medford lady — Miss Eunice Hall, who frequently saw her — Mrs. Brooks is described as "a very handsome lady, winning manners, purest blonde complexion, blue eyes, abundant pale golden hair, who wrote poetry, and sang very sweetly."

Mr. Edwin P. Whipple wrote me, —

"When I was young (about nineteen, I think) I happened to board in the same house where Mrs. Brooks resided, and had many opportunities of being acquainted, through her conversation, with the trials and disappointments of her life as a woman, and as a woman of letters. I had a great regard for her personally, and a warm admiration for her genius. . . . There was a certain sweetness and softness in her voice, which I remember; and on all topics of literature, in which she was widely versed, she was tolerant and just. I regret that I cannot find, in hunting among my papers, any review of the poems of this strangely-neglected woman of genius. I must have written many. I did all I could to extend her fame. I concurred with Dr. Griswold in all his attempts to make her striking merits as a poet admitted by her countrymen and countrywomen. It was all useless. The American people seemed to be joined in a conspiracy *not* to read 'Zóphiël,' in spite of Southey and 'The Quarterly Review,' and in spite of the endeavors of American critics who took a just pride in the genius of their countrywoman."

As woman, wife, mother, poet, and friend, in every relation of life, and in its details of dress, appearance, and manner, Maria del Occidente seems to have been a being of the most singular and attractive interest.

In 1876 I had some correspondence with the Southey family and the Coleridges. Their letters, without exception, were kind, and full of desire to assist me; but they were unable to furnish much new material.

From one of these letters, written by the Rev.

Derwent Coleridge, I quote: "Maria del Occidente does indeed deserve to be honorably remembered among the first poets of her native land. It is difficult to recover memorials of a life that is sunk beneath the stream of Lethe. A copy of her 'Zóphiël' was presented to my dear sister, Sara Coleridge, by Mr. Bancroft, the American minister, in 1834, and is now in my house." The wife of Rev. Derwent Coleridge pushed inquiry for me among the Southeys, and sent the following from Mrs. Herbert Hill, a daughter of Robert Southey: "I fear I can give no account of Mrs. Brooks that will be of any use to her biographer and friend. I have no personal recôllection of her, having been away from home during her stay at Keswick; but I well remember how full of her charms the letters were that I received from home at that time. Herbert has looked through my father's 'Life and Correspondence,' and has copied out the only thing worth stating;" which was from the "Selection of Southey's Letters," edited by J. W. Warter.

KESWICK, Oct. 13, 1833.

MY DEAR MRS. BRAY, — . . . Has "Zophiël" fallen in your way? Probably not; for books which have only their own merit to introduce them make their way slowly, if they make it at all. The authoress, who calls herself Maria del Occidente, is a widow, by name Mrs. Brooks, a New-Englander by birth, of Welsh extraction. She married, — or, to speak in this case more correctly, *was married*, — when almost a child, to a person at least thrice her own age, and as little suited to her in other respects as in years. He left her with two sons, one of whom is now an officer in the American army; the other settled as a planter in Cuba, where most of "Zóphiël" was written. Mrs. Brooks, I doubt not, always has been, and still is, haunted by the feeling, that, if she had been mated with one capable of esteeming and loving her as she deserved to be esteemed and loved, she would have been one of the happiest of God's creatures. In appearance and manners she is one of the gentlest and most feminine of women. Her poem is, in the foundation, the story of Tobias and Raguel's daughter; yet it is a most original composition, highly fanciful, and passionate in the highest degree. It has the fault of not being always perspicuous; but that any person who has read few, if any, of our elder poets, and certainly never studied any of them, nor looked upon poetry as an art, should be so free from the vices of modern diction, and possess so much of elder simplicity and beauty and strength, is most remarkable. Altogether the poem is the effusion of a heart whose fervor neither time nor untoward fortune has cooled; and of an inspiration so vivid, that it almost believes in its own creations. There is a song in the last canto which is more passionate than any I can call to mind in any language, and in my judgment far, very far, superior to Sappho's celebrated ode.

I give also, somewhat abridged, the following interesting letter from Southey's son-in-law and literary editor, the Rev. John Wood Warter, who was over seventy-one years of age at the time this quaint and readable letter was written: —

"I have deferred answering your letter till I had tried to find out if any letters of Maria del Occidente were in possession of the Southey family. By this morning's post I have a letter from my brother-in-law, the Rev. Cuthbert Southey, in which he states that there are none, adding that he well remembers her visit to Keswick. My lamented wife, Edith May Southey (Southey's eldest daughter), knew and liked her. At Southey's sale she requested me to buy the manuscript of 'Zóphiël;' which I did, and it is before me now. We received more than one little parcel from her, of guava-jelly, and two book-screens which are now on my mantelpiece. I rather suspect more is known of her than you suspect. Probably she may allude to herself in that stanza quoted in 'The Doctor.' It was generally believed that she was married, when a mere child, to an elderly man at least thrice her own age; but I have only picked this up from private letters, and can state nothing on authority. Southey often spoke of her, as did my wife, as of a gentle, pensive person, quite different from what might have been expected from the gifted and impassioned author of 'Zóphiël.' She won the regard of all the household during the few weeks of her stay at Keswick. Since I received your letter I have carefully read through 'Zóphiël' again, and think it as wonderfully clever as ever; but it was ill adapted to the English taste, which had been surfeited with 'Don Juan' and Moore. The manuscript is perhaps the greatest scrawl you ever saw. I regret I am unable to give you more information; but you may depend upon it, it is to be found either in 'Kuba' (as she pronounced Cuba), or about Matanzas. Most of my American correspondents are past and gone. The late Jared Sparks, his wife and family, visited me here some years ago. He, too, has been gathered in. He brought to my daughters autographs from Longfellow."

The following letter was written by Richard Hengist Horne in answer to inquiries about Mrs. Brooks: —

"With regard to Maria del Occidente, I perfectly recollect reading a review, in one of our quarterlies, of her poem, in conjunction with several others, most of whom seem to wither beside her burning spirit. I agree with what Southey said of her superiority to all other poetesses, my dear friend and correspondent Miss E. D. Barrett (afterward Mrs. Browning) not having appeared at that time. You are aware that the latter was also a star from the West, and either born in the West Indies, or of parents born there. I fear what you want concerning Maria Brooks is scarcely attainable now. Twenty years ago, when I went to Australia, I could probably have helped you. Miss Mitford, Mrs. Browning, Charlotte Brontë, Mrs. Hemans, and Miss Landon (L. E. L.), could most likely have told you more or less of Mrs. Brooks. So could Jordan (of 'The Gazette'), Leigh Hunt, Robert Bell, and others; but, alas! all these and more young literary friends are gone. By the by, it is possible that in Bell's edition of the 'British Poets' you may find her mentioned. In case you have not the work, I will look into it the next time I am in the British-Museum Library; and, if there be any thing worth copying out, I will send it to you. Tennyson and Browning may have known something of her."

Later he adds, —

"I enclose Browning's reply with regard to Mrs. Brooks: 'As to Maria del Occidente, I know the name, but never remember hearing it from my wife. You revive old impressions in me that there is real worth in her poetry, judging from the echoes rather than the veritable voice, which I never heard; and I wonder that I can give you no sort of account of the lady.'"

In this letter Mr. Horne very kindly sent a charming sonnet, never before published, which, especially in its closing lines, is in deep sympathy with the abrupt catastrophe of "Idomen;" and for this reason I have selected it as being peculiarly tender and fitting for the inscription-page of this volume. My paper on "Maria del Occidente" (of which the present writing is in part a reconstruction) in the "Harper's Magazine" for January, giving Mr. Horne's sonnet shorter by one line than it now appears, elicited from him a very kind letter, enclosing a revision of the sonnet with the missing line supplied; concerning which I cannot forbear quoting, somewhat at my own expense: "You will be amused when I tell you the cause of this additional line originated in your use of a word intended for what the Spaniards and Italians would call an 'affectionate diminutive,'—i.e., my 'charming little sonnet.' As all sonnets should be conventionally of the same size, I was suddenly induced to count the lines, and discovered that what I had intended as a kind of elegiac sister to your 'Maria del Occidente' had lost one leg! Perhaps I did not call it a sonnet!" But he did!

Early in 1876 I made one more appeal to Col. Brooks, reiterating my desire for the possession of his mother's papers. He replied that no one but himself could possibly find them if any existed; that since her death he had "been through the old Mexican war, the new Mexican war, the Kansas war, and the Rebellion: so you can imagine what changes have taken place, and how my effects are scattered. I gave a copy of 'Zóphiël' to Adjutant-Gen. Townsend, who will lend it to you, I think. If I go East this summer, I will endeavor to look up her papers; but I still doubt if any thing of importance could be found. You must know that I feel very grateful to you," &c.

On my application for it, Gen. E. D. Townsend at once placed his copy of "Zóphiël" at my disposal.

"Zóphiël, or The Bride of Seven," is an Oriental epic. The foundation is the story of Sara, Raguel's daughter, of the Median city of Ecbatane, as given in the fifth, sixth, and seventh chapters of the book of Tobit, in the Apocrypha. Sara, a beautiful and good maiden, is bitterly reproached because "she had been married to seven husbands, whom Asmodeus, the evil spirit, had killed before they had lien with her." Unhappy in being the cause of so many deaths, and suffering from the reproaches, Sara prays for death, but that, if she must continue to live, some mercy and pity may be shown her. In answer to this prayer the angel Raphaël was sent to bring Tobias to the house of Raguel, where Sara should be given to him to be his wife. Nothing daunted by the father's confession concerning Sara's seven bridegrooms, Tobias entreats for an immediate marriage; and, the evil spirit Asmodeus being overcome by a peculiar spell, the predestined nuptials take place. Upon this foundation the author of "Zóphiël" enlarges, mingling the dramatic movement, situations, and passionate climaxes created by her own affluent imagination, with the rich imagery and action of ancient myth.

With the threefold quality of the highest order of genius, the intuitive, perceptive, and creative, she detaches whatever she uses from its original source, and so imbues it with her own meaning, so individualizes it with her own inspiration, that it enters into a new crystallization.

The plot of the poem clearly indicates its author's purpose, — to show how the passion of love affects individual fate, moulding and swaying both human and angelic nature. The scenery of the drama is painted, the characters are chosen, the circumstances for their development selected, to this end; and no expression of individual opinion however appreciative, and no review or criticism however capable, can be so adequate an act of justice as the republication of the poem itself. For those lovers of literature who have not leisure for its more studious pursuit I have prepared the following prose sketch of the scenes and movement of "Zóphiël," in the hope that it may be a welcome facilitation to their understanding and enjoyment of its beauties.

The author's notes to "Zóphiël," which are well worth reading, independent of the beautiful poem they elucidate, — and which were originally printed not only in groups at the close of each canto, but scattered through the cantos themselves, the text being plentifully defaced with asterisks, daggers, and numerals, — have been re-arranged, and placed by themselves at the close of the book, with such designation of page, verse, and line, as will not only enable the reader to find any passage referred to with facility, but, when found, to enjoy it free from the intrusiveness of mechanical signs.

Concerning these notes I quote from the preface of the original edition: —

"One or two short articles in journals of this country object to this poem as being difficult to understand; but those who make the objection probably read it hastily, and confused themselves by looking from the verses to the notes, and back again, thus distracting the attention. It will be better to read the story as it was composed, without reference to explanations or comments till the whole is finished. The notes can be read afterwards with equal advantage. Indeed, they are merely added to show how much authority exists for every incident and allusion of a narrative imagined under the influence of soft luxuriant tropical scenery, where the writer drew solely from nature, and had access to no books at all relative to the subject. 'Zóphiël,' if read in the manner proposed, will be found as simply arranged, and as easy to comprehend, as the tales of 'Arabian Nights,' or any common novel."

For my own part, I would suggest that the notes to one canto at a time should be read *first*, and *without* alternately looking from the verse to the notes, and thereafter the canto to which the notes so read refer; and I think it will be found that the delicate significances and shades of meaning thus imparted to the *first* reading of each canto will richly repay the reader's care.

The Asmodeus, Raguel, Sara, Raphaël, and Tobias of the apocryphal story are respectively the *Zóphiël*, Zorah, Egla, Hariph, and Helon of the poem.

"Zóphiël" opens with a strange appeal, in a mood both brave and desolate. As in mournful prescience of the lack of wide recognition she was to experience, the singer, from the solitude of her little temple, salutes the "shade of Columbus," her Cymbrian ancestors, the bards of Mona, and the "spirits who hovered o'er the Euphrates stream" before the first waking of Eve, seeming to entreat an audience of these.

The first canto, "A Grove of Acacias," contains something of the argument of the whole poem, introduces the "bride of seven," and gives the first act in the sixfold tragedy.

One day, while Egla is reclining in the grove, she is joined by her mother Sephora, who entreats Egla to choose a husband, or to permit one to be chosen for her. Egla, in reply, tells Sephora of the visit of an old man in the wood (the same who appears under the name *Hariph* in the progress of the poem), who foretold to her the bridegroom who would one day come to her from the Euphrates, impressing his prophecy by revealing himself as the angel Raphaël for an instant before vanishing. Sephora discredits not Egla, but the vision; dreads the fading of Egla's youth and beauty, and beseeches her not to waste them upon a "thought-love."

Egla yields a sorrowful yet gentle obedience to her mother's persuasions, and is left to sleep in her acacian bower.

Into the Lethean hush of these Persian woods enters *Zóphiël*, a fallen but powerful angel, the most majestic conception of this poem. He sees the faint flame where Zorah, Egla's father, sacrifices in the wood; and, brooding over the lost joys of heaven, he apostrophizes ambition in a strong outburst of eloquent despair. Approaching the bower, and believing that he sees a "faithful angel" in the beautiful sleeper, he turns to depart, but is arrested by a sigh from Egla; perceives that she is but a mortal maiden, though so fair; and in the yearning of his naturally loving soul, intensified by banishment, resolves to win her love for himself.

At length, on the night set apart for the marriage of Egla with Meles, the reluctant girl retires to her chamber, and prays for a submissive spirit to do her parents' will. From this melancholy devotion she is roused by the coming of Zóphiël, who, revealing his supernal beauty, entreats for her confidence with every exquisite art of tenderness; but Egla, by pure virginal instinct, detects treachery in Zóphiël's appeal, resists his powerful spell, and re-affirms her acceptance of Meles in obedience to her parents. Zóphiël vanishes, and Meles enters, only to be mysteriously slain at the bridal bedside.

Neither in "The Loves of the Angels" nor in "Lalla Rookh" does Thomas Moore's flowing measure equal the musical cadences of "Zóphiël;" and there is greater beauty of scene and bloom lavished on the single acacian bower where Zóphiël wistfully watches over Egla's sleep than on the whole journey of the beautiful Lalla. In the

Choric Song of Tennyson's "Lotos-Eaters," the mosaic detail of sensuous description, though as delicate, is not so thoughtful, nor so warm in feeling.

Sardius, the young king of Media, learning the manner of his favorite Meles' death, detains Egla in his palace in strict but kind restraint, which is jealously observed by Philomars. This character, limned in three verses, is one of the darkest and strongest pictures of the human fiend to be found in literature.

Egla's dress, when sent for to "evening banquet" with King Sardius, is something more than a superb festal toilet: it is the artistic expression of her nature and situation, modestly yet consciously chosen by her to be such. In every scene, under every test, Egla's charm is one with her goodness, and every soul that is moved by her beauty is moved higher.

Byron and Swinburne have a language-magic something like that in which this toilet[1] and banquet scene are described; but neither so infuse their description of woman's beauty with that intenser loveliness of the spirit which makes the body the breath and picture of the soul. In the second canto, after several gay courtiers have dared and met the doom of Meles, at the threshold of Egla's chamber, Altheëtor, a very beautiful

1 See Canto Second, pp. 53, 54.

youth of Sardius' court, of a nature pure and high as it is ardent, falls ill, pines secretly for Egla, and becomes another victim of Zóphiël's jealous wrath.

In the third and fourth cantos, "Palace of the Gnomes" and "The Storm," we have a description of celestial and inframundane scenery and drama, and the spiritual proportions of Zóphiël come into full relief.

In the first scene of "The Palace of the Gnomes" Zóphiël and Phraërion sit conversing among the moonlighted ruins on the banks of the lotos-broidered Tigris. The description of the scene around them is delicate as an ivory-painting, and bright and iris-tinted as that structure of aërial fancies, "The House of Clouds."[1]

The characters of Zóphiël and Phraërion are contrasted with an admirable penetration; Phraërion being the beautiful, gentle, languid spirit, to whom the haunts of the most rare and fragrant flowers and dews, and the secrets of their precious distillations, are known. In nothing but the softness of love is he a companion for the strong, restless, suffering Zóphiël; but the latter, formed for intensest love and friendship, and bereft of heaven and its companionships, in his loneliness draws the mild Phraërion to him by the little link of love

[1] Mrs. E. B. Browning.

that is possible to their differing natures, and cherishes him with that pathetic fidelity which is conscious of giving an ocean in exchange for a rill. Nevertheless, this complex and very human Zóphiël coerces the pleasure-loving, shrinking Phraërion to serve him by conducting him through all the tortures and horrors of a subterranean journey; for these spirits are formed to feel unspeakable pangs from ordinary contact with material substances of earth and wave.

At the submarine palace of the gnome Tàhathyam Zóphiël obtains a crystal spar, in which one drop of the elixir which perpetuates life is enclosed.

With this between his lips, and his fragile guide Phraërion clasped to his breast, he sets out to return from the sea-deeps to the earth's surface. The most violent submarine storm engages all his supernatural powers; and the precious spar, — containing the potent crystal drop which is to perpetuate for Zóphiël the youth and beauty of Egla, — for the possession of which so much has been endured, is dashed from his lips, and whelmed in an ocean-gulf, into whose vortex he may not plunge without remaining an eternity. The two storm-spent sprites emerge "near Lybia's coast," only to encounter a terrific earth-storm, in whose relentless fury Zóphiël perceives the malignant purpose of an evil spirit more powerful than himself. He lends all his strength and care to shelter the delicate Phraërion ; but at last, in the storm's climax, both are dashed "prostrate on the sands."

Though there are glimpses of the "Inferno" in "Zóphiël," the story does not lead through its scenes. Yet the great likeness in kind and quality between the genius of the "melancholy Florentine" and that revealed in "Zóphiël" could not escape the student of both poets. In scope and plot the "Inferno" and "Zóphiël" are scarcely to be compared: there is too much unlikeness of attempt. But the soul-current vitalizing each of these poems is the warm and brilliant, passionate and profound, tide of a like inspiration. In the plot of "Zóphiël" the stream flows necessarily between nearer banks, but proves its identity of source by the floating flower, the golden sand, the tint and depth and lustre that flow from no lesser springs.

In the tenth canto of the "Inferno," the discourse between Dante and "Farinata degli Uberti" and Cavalcanti, and the accessories of the situation, are, in their dark sublimity, wonderfully like the scene of recrimination between Zóphiël and the fiend in "The Storm," though the likeness is in the power and feeling rather than in the situation.

It is in "The Storm" (fourth canto) that the genius of Milton is matched in quality, if not in scope, and his Satan is distanced by the spiritual majesty of Zóphiël and the "sombre being" who copes with him in the tempest. Here is no effort to impress with physical loathsomeness and horror; here is stature, but with concealing robe; a sombre presence of mystic power and beauty, infused with evil, and impressive by the distinctively spiritual significance of the vision. In the first book of "Paradise Lost," Milton's presentment of Satan, though a grand is a somewhat coarse appeal to our physical perceptions of the horrible. He lies upon the burning flood, serpent in form, a coiling bulk of horrors, "floating many a rood." This startles and oppresses. The impressiveness of spiritual power, when for evil, lies in the obscuring of the physical bulk and deformity; in the veiled mystery from which projects the vague, incalculable dark essence and malignant intent.

In the eighth book of "Paradise Lost" a common and low conception of love's passion is suggested to Adam by angelic lips, which is redeemed by a counter utterance of the same angel a little farther on. But, in Zóphiël himself, — though fallen from his angelic state, and therefore less perfect than Adam before his fall, — love has an ideally pure expression. Though he slays Egla's bridegrooms, he is eager to dare and do and suffer to the limits of his nature's vast endowments, only for the sake of preserving and blessing the charming being whom he cannot hope to embrace,—the simplest, innocent movement of whose breast is watched by him with reverence. In book ninth of "Paradise Lost," Satan's "compassing the earth," though a more comprehensive journey, is told less impressively, and with less of poetic beauty, than is the similar but shorter journey of Zóphiël and Phraërion to the palace of the Gnome.

After the conflict between the spirits in "The Storm" is past, Zóphiël seeks Phraërion in his covert. Embracing, they rise into the air, and, mantling themselves in the morning mists, flee toward Media to Egla's grove. Beneath them, as they pass, two travellers by the Tigris pause in delighted wonder at the sweet odors which the flight of the unseen spirits has fanned from many fields of flowers.

These travellers are the youth Helon, and Hariph (the angel Raphaël),—the same who, in the disguise of an old man, foretold her bridegroom to Egla in her acacian retreat, and now in this same disguise is leading Helon, unawares, to his predestined bride. As (in the beginning of the fifth canto, "Zameïa") they converse together,

Helon relates a dream of the preceding night, which saddens him with vague longing, in which he saved from fearful and imminent death a maiden of celestial grace and beauty. The incidents of this dream are afterward realized between him and Egla in the sixth canto.

As they journey on they come upon a remarkable group resting beneath a projecting rock. These are the Princess Zameïa (the fugitive wife of white-haired, polygamic, pagan Imlec), her slave Neantes, and a little Ethiop boy. Zameïa is sleeping, drugged by the compassionate Neantes. She is portrayed as travel-worn and passion-wasted, but marvellously beautiful still, with the dark charm of Syrian women. While she sleeps, Neantes relates the history of her first meeting with Meles while making sacrifice at the fanes of Mylitta, the Assyrian Venus, according to the Babylonian custom; of the instant and lasting love she conceived for him; of their secret meetings in her palace by the Euphrates, where Meles climbs her garden-wall by means of a ladder woven of her silken girdles. There is all the tenderness, and passionate self-immolation to love, of Romeo and Juliet, between these lovers; only that Zameïa is sincere, while Meles seeks only himself in seeking her, and warily takes care of himself, and soon forsakes. Zameïa, in despair, wastes almost unto death, until Neantes prepares a letter which is to deceive Zameïa into supposing that Meles is detained on embassy by the king, but will return by "the gathering of the date." Twice Neantes resorts to this deception in order to save her life and reason. At last Zameïa hears from Imlec the news that he is returning, and would have her prepare to receive him. Frantic between her starved, despairing love for absent Meles and her loathing for the returning Imlec, she, with Neantes, departs by night, casting some of her clipt black tresses braided with jewels into the Euphrates, that it may lead to the idea of her death by drowning.

The description of the temple and rites of Mylitta is identical in fact with the same related by Herodotus, Guignant, and others; but in the verse of "Zóphiël" it is so refined of the commoner conceptions of such a rite, and is invested with so much seriousness and beauty as having an impersonal and simply sacrificial significance, that merely sensual appreciation must recoil chilled as from the pure nakedness of a statue. The whole movement of this canto, its glow and form and finish, are as replete with beauty as the richest measures of Byron when Byron's impulse was — as it sometimes was — noble and pure, and is wholly without the trail of reckless license that creeps through some of his fairest creations. The limpid flowing song of Mrs. Browning's "Swan's Nest among the Reeds" is recalled, not by any analogy of scope or *motif;* but the soft and vivid delicacy of feeling and expression is the same.

The yet unsubsided wave of what has gone before, and the imminence of the last crisis, is immediately felt in the first verses of "The Bridal of Helon" (the sixth and last canto), where occurs the ardent complaint which Southey quotes with such admiring delight in "The Doctor."

Egla, in the soft twilight solitude of her acacia-grove, muses as she tunes her lute, longing for Zóphiël's presence:—

"Softly heaving
The while her heart, thus from its inmost core
Such feelings gushed, to Lydian numbers weaving,
As never had her lip expressed before:—

SONG OF EGLA.

Day in melting purple dying,
Blossoms all around me sighing,
Fragrance from the lilies straying,
Zephyr with my ringlets playing,
Ye but waken my distress:
I am sick of loneliness.

Thou to whom I love to hearken,
Come ere night around me darken:

Though thy softness but deceive me,
Say thou'rt true, and I'll believe thee.
  Veil, if ill, thy soul's intent:
  Let me think it innocent!

Save thy toiling; spare thy treasure:
All I ask is friendship's pleasure:
Let the shining ore lie darkling;
Bring no gem in lustre sparkling;
  Gifts and gold are nought to me:
  I would only look on thee;

Tell to thee the high-wrought feeling,
Ecstasy but in revealing;
Paint to thee the deep sensation,
Rapture in participation,
  Yet but torture, if comprest
  In a lone, unfriended breast.

Absent still? Ah, come and bless me!
Let these eyes again caress thee.
Once, in caution, I could fly thee:
Now I nothing could deny thee.
  In a look if death there be,
  Come, and I will gaze on thee!"

Southey declared this poem to be not only equal, but superior, to Sappho's famous "Ode to Aphrodite." There is in places a strange likeness of emotion and power in the two ardent adjurations. Here is the Sapphic hymn as the New-England poet-philosopher, Thomas Wentworth Higginson, gracefully translates it:—

"Beautiful, throned, immortal Aphrodite!
Daughter of Zeus! beguiler, I implore thee
Weigh me not down with weariness and anguish,
O thou most holy!

Come to me now, if ever thou in kindness
Hearkenedst my words; and often hast thou hearkened,
Heeding, and coming from the mansions golden
Of thy great Father,

Yoking thy chariots, borne by thy most lovely
Consecrated birds, with dusky-tinted pinions,
Waving swift wings from utmost heights of heaven,
Through the mid ether:

Swiftly they vanished, leaving thee, O goddess!
Smiling, with face immortal in its beauty,
Asking what I suffered, and why in utter longing
I had dared call thee;

Asking what I sought thus hopeless in desiring,
'Wildered in brain, and spreading nets of passion,
Alas! for whom? and saidst thou, 'Who has harmed thee,
O my poor Sappho?

'Though now he flies, ere long he shall pursue;
Fearing thy gifts, he too, in turn, shall bring them:
Loveless to-day, to-morrow he shall woo thee,
Though thou shouldst spurn him.'

Thus seek me now, O holy Aphrodite!
Save me from anguish; give me all I wish for,—
Gifts at thy hand; and thine shall be the glory,
Sacred protector!"

Thus Sappho, praying to love's source; while Egla entreats only a lover: yet Egla's song is tenderer music. Sappho desires gifts, her own happiness, and to be love-compelling: Egla seeks only permission to completely love and bless. Her passion and its prayer are diviner than Sappho's, and the song which breathes them is a more penetrating strain, reminding of the tender human woe of the foreboding Willow Song of Desdemona, and the lily maid of Astolat's Song of Love and Death.

A guardian spirit, perceiving the dangerous situation of Egla, hovers near her at the same moment that Zóphiël, just returning from the fruitless subterranean journey and storm-conflict related in the third and fourth cantos, approaches her; listens in transport to the song; at whose close, with tender sighs, she breathes his name. At this moment, when Zóphiël is about to reveal himself, Zameïa, crazed with jealous hatred of Egla on account of the desertion and death of Meles, darts forward, and falls dead in the attempt to kill Egla.

Forced to witness at her very feet Zameïa's passionate death, and weary of the long scene of horrors of which she is the innocent cause, Egla prepares to take her own life. Helon, her predestined bridegroom, frustrates her design. Their betrothal follows. Zóphiël, while this transpires, is withheld in the wood in vain struggle with the "dark Being of the Storm," but escapes, and reaches Egla's bridal chamber only in time to be repelled by the "insufferable perfume fire" of the burning contents of the carneol box, given long ago to Helon, for the protection of this very hour, by Hariph, who hurls the wretched Zóphiël away, and discloses himself to the bridal pair as the angel Raphaël.

Raphaël then seeks Zóphiël with wish and word of heavenly pity, consolation, and hope.

The review of this poem at the time of its appearance, both in England and America, did what seemed like a reluctant sort of justice. Though the ocean rolled between us and the mother-country, and though by every principle of government, national hope and endeavor, we were sharply divided from her, still our gods in literature had been and were her gods, — Shakspeare, Spenser, and Milton. A country with a young civilization and a young literature, we did not expect and were not prepared to meet a revelation of American genius ranking with the great poets of the world. Even Mr. Griswold, the personal friend and admirer of Maria del Occidente, waited for the English verdict before speaking half his mind.

The faults found in "Zóphiël" were notably of that class which are blemishes or charms according to the mental temperament impressed. It was inevitably subjected to coarse as well as to noble interpretation; yet the least sympathetic appreciation acknowledged its greatness and distinctive originality, while a certain element peculiar to a past era in British criticism was curiously betrayed in an uncomfortable astonishment, a sort of blank and vexed amazement, that so majestic a strain could have risen in skies that did not immediately arch over Shakspeare's isle. "And all this," said "The London Quarterly," in closing a short but keen tribute of admiration, "out of a coffee-plantation in Cuba!"

From Maria del Occidente's miscellaneous works two only are selected for this volume,—"The Ode to the Departed," written to her son Edgar, and one of the most heroically tender lamentations ever written; and "The Farewell to Cuba," which has the grace and coloring of a tropic flower.

In speaking of "Zóphiël," Mr. Griswold says, "Zóphiël seems to us the finest fallen angel that has come to us from the hand of a poet. Milton's outcasts from heaven are utterly depraved, and abraded of their glory; but Zóphiël has traces of his original virtue and beauty, and a lingering hope of restoration to the presence of the Divinity." He adds, "There were, at the time of the publication of 'Zóphiël' in Boston (1834), too few readers among us of sufficiently cultivated and independent taste to appreciate a work of art which time or accident had not commended to the popular applause. At the end of a month, only about twenty copies had been sold; and, in a moment of disappointment, Mrs. Brooks caused the remainder of the impression to be withdrawn from the market. This poem has, therefore, been very little read in this country; and even the title of it would have remained unknown to the common reader of elegant literature but for occasional allusions to it by Southey and other foreign critics."

Being desirous of having a full edition of her works, including "Idomen," published, Mrs. Brooks authorized Mr. Griswold to "offer gratuitously her copyrights to an eminent publishing-house for that purpose. In the existing condition of the *copyright laws, which should have been entitled 'Acts for the Discouragement of a Native Literature,'* she was not surprised that the offer was declined, though indignant that the reason assigned should have been that they were 'of too elevated a character to sell.'"

Writing to Mr. Griswold soon afterward, she observed, "I do not think any thing from my humble imagination can be *too elevated,* or elevated enough, for the public as it really is in these North-American States. . . . In the words of poor Spurzheim, uttered to me a short time before his death in Boston, I solace myself by saying, 'Stupidity! stupidity! the knowledge of that alone has saved me from misanthropy.'"

In 1844, about a year before her death, she wrote to Mr. Griswold, "When I have written out my 'Vistas del Infierno' and one other short poem, I hope to begin the penning of the epic of which I have so often spoken to you, — 'Beatriz, the Beloved of Columbus;' but when or whether it will be finished, Heaven alone can tell."

In allusion to this letter, Mr. Griswold says, "I have not learned whether this poem was written; but, when I heard her repeat passages of it, I thought it would be a nobler work than 'Zóphiël.'"

At the time of her death (in 1845) Mr. Griswold wrote, "She was one of the most remarkable women that ever lived. To great attainments in literature she joined a powerful and original genius, and a character of singular energy and individuality. Both in England and the United States, she has been considered, by those who have read her writings thoughtfully, as unmatched among poets of her sex.

"'Zóphiël' is one of the few compositions destined for durable fame. It is one of the most original, passionate, and harmonious works of imagination ever conceived; and there breathes through the whole the vital life of genius.

"Silently and surely her genius will work its way into the great public heart, and her fame grow with time; and I cannot conceive of the period when an American, reviewing the causes which have conduced to place his country in a proud intellectual position, and assisted in giving to it the immortality which springs from literature, shall cease to regard with peculiar gratitude and admiration the name of the authoress of 'Zóphiël.'"

Yet embarking solely upon its own merits, without herald and without plaudit, this great poem, receiving but a brief salute, was suffered to pass, as a ship sets sail, into the mists of obscurity, and, fading from sight, to fade even from remembrance. But at last, let us hope, those mists are parted, and the waters of her native shores shall lap, with waves of welcome and sweet loudening recognition, the long-hidden bark.

In a letter expressing cordial sympathy with my work, and great pleasure at the republication of Mrs. Brooks's poems, my beloved friend, Mr. John Greenleaf Whittier, says, "When a young man, I read 'Zóphiël,'—a most remarkable poem,—and have never forgotten it. The impassioned song which Southey praised so highly is a perfect gem.

If 'Zóphiël' is *published now*, it will be appreciated as it deserves to be."

The authoress of "Zóphiël" wrote one prose tale, — "Idomen; or, The Vale of Yumuri." Its scenery is tropical and Cuban, — a glowing bit of tapestry upon which the action is wrought in rich but more sombre tints.

Mr. Griswold, who was her personal friend, and probably knew her private history, declares, "'Idomen' contains little that is fictitious except the names of the characters. The account which Idomen gives of her own history is *literally true*, except in relation to an excursion to Niagara, which occurred, but in a different period of the author's life. 'Idomen' will possess an interest and value as a psychological study independent of that which belongs to it as a *record of the experience* of so eminent a poet."

My own research has shown me that it is undoubtedly autobiographical, and in some sense a confession; and in this light it cannot be read but with the deepest sympathy and reverent interest. The same great capacity for intense, passionate devotion of love, which animates her verse, is revealed in this little heart-history; and there is the same evidence of a grandly-endowed nature undergoing almost complete spiritual deprivation in an uncongenial companionship.

As a psychological study, and as a work of art, "Idomen" has a beauty and separateness such as attaches to Allston's "Monaldi," to Moore's "Epicurean," to the "Atala" of Châteaubriand, or to "Vathek," the "Sorrows of Werther," and "Paul and Virginia."

Since the foregoing was written, I have had the good fortune to learn further particulars of the personal history of Maria del Occidente, which will be given in my forthcoming edition of "Idomen" (now in press), and which corroborate Mr. Griswold's statement as to its autobiographical character.

ZADEL BARNES GUSTAFSON.

FEBRUARY, 1879.

PREFACE

TO THE SECOND AMERICAN EDITION.

(*Published for the benefit of the Polish Exiles.*)

BOSTON: HILLIARD, GRAY, & CO., 1834.

IT is now more than three years since this poem was prepared for the press; and while employed about its notes, in Paris, during the winter immediately succeeding the late Revolution, the writer conceived a design of publishing it as a slight assistance to the Polish cause, — a cause at that time so fashionable, that private ladies of rank and character performed at public concerts for the purpose of increasing a fund for the oppressed but "nobles Polonais." On the evening of the 2d of March, 1831, such a concert was attended, and the tickets sold for a napoleon each. Praiseworthy as it was, alas that such a cause should have required such assistance!

Poland fell; and the fashion of befriending her, like other fashions, soon passed away. "It is of no use," said almost every one, "to try and befriend a country that is entirely fallen." But how can a country be no more while her children still exist? or how can a cause be extinct while those who engaged in defending it are still alive, and still willing to struggle? Men there are who come thousands of miles to an unknown country, and endure all the misery and scorn that attend poverty and dependence, rather than to join the armies of their oppressors, or than even to use their swords as mere mercenaries against nations that never wronged them.

Whatever may be the future fate of magnanimous but betrayed Poland, many of her persecuted defenders *suffer* for the necessaries of life in the bosom of this prosperous community. The feeling awakened by their arrival has burned for a moment. May it not pass away like a flame of straw kindled on a rock!

The arrival of Polish exiles will soon cease to be a novelty; but it is melancholy to reflect that their sufferings and wants must continue. To be able to relieve even the slightest of such afflictions will be sufficient compensation to the composer of the following cantos.

It is the design of the writer to get out as many editions, *for the purpose already said*, as she can find either means or friends to engage in; but how many that will be rests at present with the great Director of human and individual circumstance.

It may be well to mention here, that the labor of the publisher is undertaken on reasonable terms. The present edition consists of five hundred copies. After every expense is paid, a balance of two hundred and fifty dollars, or perhaps rather more, will remain at the disposal of the Polish Committee: that is, if all the copies are purchased; if gentlemen possessed both of humanity, and a love for the fine arts, are willing to give (either for the poem or the object of its publication) the same small sum so often paid for the spectacle of a new melodrama, or the airs of a musical *débutante*.

For those (and of such certainly there are many) who are diffident of their own opinion, and dislike to purchase or even to read a book unless previously and highly recommended, it may not be amiss to observe that no poetical work ever written in the New World has received greater praise in Europe than the Oriental story, or poem, now presented. In proof of this assertion, passages from popular English works, as well as many private letters, can be brought forward if necessary.[1]

There was a time when every Roman artist was content to rest his reputation on Grecian taste and encomiums. Such a time is still present to Americans in regard to their "Alma Mater," at least so far as concerns either poetry, painting, sculpture, architecture, or music.

The elms and oaks of liberty and utility are growing so strong and fast in this rich land of corn and forest-trees, that little sun or moisture can be spared for "arts, a tribe of sensitives." When any aspirant or artist, therefore, believes himself possessed of the power of imitating his Creator by giving material semblance to forms already existing in his own "world of ideas," he generally succeeds in reaching the other continent, the land of his forefathers; and on the approbation obtained in that

[1] A very favorable notice appeared last autumn (soon after Zóphiël appeared in London) in Fraser's Magazine. A late work called The Doctor, reviewed in the British Quarterly, mentions Zóphiël, or the Bride of Seven, as the "most passionate and imaginative of any poem ever written by a female."

land depends in a great degree his future success and reputation. As instances of this may be mentioned Benjamin West, Greenough, and, indeed (with few exceptions), every American who has distinguished himself either by forms of beauty or the embodiment of beautiful conceptions.

To return a moment to the poem in question: Mr. Southey and others think it will take a permanent place among such English works as are thought worth preserving: if that should be the case, it will probably owe its preservation to the nature and treatment of its subject; or, in other words, to its originality.

Châteaubriand, in his noble poem "Les Martyrs," has introduced angels as presiding over the various passions of his enchanting mortals; but, in English, Milton, Byron, and Moore are, it is believed, all who have attempted to depict those sometimes erring yet celestial messengers as existing in friendly intercourse with beings of earth. From neither of these masters is "Zóphiël" a copy.

MARIA GOWEN BROOKS.

ADVERTISEMENT.

Any member of the Polish Committee, or competent agent for the relief of suffering Polish exiles, can see the exact amount of the expenses of publication from an estimate made by Messrs. Hilliard, Gray, & Co.; and, provided such an agent will dispose of any specified number of volumes, he can retain an overplus of at least half he receives for the immediate relief of such as it is intended to benefit.

NOTE TO THE SECOND EDITION.

It was thought by a friend of the Polish sufferers, who was so good as to interest himself in the publication of this work, that *some* religious persons might object to the following stanza, which occurs near the beginning of the first canto: —

" Blest were those days! Can these dull ages boast
Aught to compare? Though now no more beguile,
Chained in their darkling depths, the infernal host,
Who would not brave a fiend to share an angel's smile?

The reader is requested to consider these lines as merely the expression of a passing emotion, occasioned by a sudden thought of the exquisite pleasure that must be felt in looking, if it were possible, at a creature entirely superior to mortals, and coming from the abodes of perfection.

M. G. B.

PREFACE.

In finishing "Zóphiël," the writer has endeavored to adhere entirely to that belief (once prevalent among the fathers of the Greek and Roman churches) which supposes that the oracles of antiquity were delivered by demons or fallen angels, who wandered about the earth, formed attachments to such mortals as pleased them best, and caused themselves, in many places, to be adored as divinities.

In endeavoring to give authority for the incidents of the story, all quotations from the sacred writings have been scrupulously avoided; and the beings introduced are to be considered only as Phœbus, Zephyr, &c., under other names.

Most of the systems of ancient philosophy, either Western or Oriental, suppose beings similar to the angels of the fathers, and differ from the Mosaic account only in being more full and explicit. Justin Martyr and others supposed that even Homer borrowed from Hebraic records and traditions, and found in his writings the creation of the world, the Tower of Babel, and the angels cast out of heaven. Hesiod's beautiful allegory of "Love calling order from chaos "[1] may, it is said, be traced to the same source.

The fact of the actual existence of such beings as angels, it is for others to question: according to all that is related of them, they are creatures superior in power, but endued with wishes and propensities nearly resembling those of mortals; and, in their attributes, corresponding almost entirely with those deities which they are thought by the fathers to have pérsonated, and which have ever been a subject for poetry and fable.

M. G. B.

[1] *Vide* Brucker's Historia Philosophiæ.

TO

ROBERT SOUTHEY, ESQ.

O LAURELLED bard! how can I part,
  Those cheering smiles no more to see,
Until my soothed and solaced heart
  Pours forth one grateful lay to thee?

Fair virtue tuned thy youthful breath,
  And peace and pleasure bless thee now;
For love and beauty guard the wreath
  That blooms upon thy manly brow.

The Indian leaning on his bow,
  On hostile cliff, in desert drear,
Cast with less joy his glance below
  When came some friendly warrior near;

The native dove of that warm isle
  Where oft with flowers my lyre was drest,
Sees with less joy the sun a while
  When vertic rains have drenched her nest,—

Than I, a stranger, first beheld
  Thine eye's harmonious welcome given
With gentle word, which, as it swelled,
  Came to my heart benign as heaven.

Soft be thy sleep as mists that rest
  On Skiddaw's top at summer morn!
Smooth be thy days as Derwent's breast
  When summer light is almost gone!

And yet for thee why breathe a prayer?
  I deem thy fate is given in trust
To seraphs, who by daily care
  Would prove that Heaven is not unjust.

And treasured shall thine image be
  In memory's purest, holiest shrine,
While truth and honor glow in thee,
  Or life's warm quivering pulse is mine.

MARIA GOWEN BROOKS.

KESWICK, April 18, 1831.

SONNET

TO THE MEMORY OF

MARIA DEL OCCIDENTE.

BY THE AUTHOR OF "ORION."

WE gaze into blue depths of Western skies,
Where Cuba sleeps 'neath stars and starlike suns:
The splendor brims and overfills our eyes,
Till earth's dark sandglass stops, or scarcely runs.
We note, amidst the host, one special light:
Our thoughts then melt toward the eternal Giver
Of pure infinitude to mortal sight:
We look again; *that* light is gone forever!
Where hath it gone? where hath its glory fled?
Is the world struck with blindness, or with error?
Who saw it as we saw it? what delight or terror
Can picture its bright throne among the dead?
Alas for that soul's fire! — lost, shot astray,
Leaving few records in our night or day!

RICHARD HENGIST HORNE.

SEPT. 12, 1872.

“ZÓPHIËL;

OR,

THE BRIDE OF SEVEN.”

CANTO FIRST.

GROVE OF ACACIAS.

ZÓPHIËL.

GROVE OF ACACIAS.

I.

SHADE of Columbus ! here thy relics rest ;
  Here, while these numbers to the desert ring,
The selfsame breeze that passes o'er thy breast
  Salutes me as with panting heart I sing.

II.

Madoc ! my ancient fathers' bones repose
  Where their bold harps thy country's bards inwreathed ;
And this warm blood once coursed the veins of those
  Who flourished where thy first faint sigh was breathed.

III.

Heroes departed both ! if still ye love
  These realms to which on earth ye oped the way,
Amid the joys that crown your deeds above
  One moment pause, and deign to bless my lay.

IV.

Spirits who hovered o'er Euphrates' stream
 When the first beauteous mother of our race
First oped her mild eyes to the new light-beam,
 And in the lucid wave first saw her own fair face,

Did then yon ocean in its bosom press
 These western solitudes? or are they new
Only to men? Was this sweet wilderness,
 This distant world, then visited by you?

V.

If ye then knew, or haply if ye here
 Come wandering now, oh, listen! nor refuse
Your unseen harps a moment to my ear.
 Of one like you I'd sing: whisper my trembling Muse!

VI.

Rest in my wild retreat! The solar fires
 Tell on this glowing cheek their fervid powers;
Yet 'tis the ocean's breath my lip respires,
 Grown fragrant in its course o'er thousand shrubs and
 flowers.

VII.

The time has been — this holiest records tell —
 When restless spirits raised a war in heaven.
Great was the crime; and, banished thence, they fell
 To depths unknown, yet kept the potence, given

For nobler use, to tempt the hapless race
  Of feeble mortals, who but form a grade
'Twixt spirits and the courser of the chase.
  Man, thing of heaven and earth, why thou wert made

Ev'n spirits knew not; yet they loved to sport
  With thy mysterious mind, and lent their powers
The good to benefit, the ill to hurt.
  Dark fiends assailed thee in thy dangerous hours;

But better angels thy far perils eyed,
  And often, when in heaven they might have staid,
Came down to watch by some just hero's side,
  Or meet the aspiring love of some high-gifted maid.

VIII.

Blest were those days! Can these dull ages boast
  Aught to compare? Though now no more beguile,
Chained in their darkling depths, the infernal host,
  Who would not brave a fiend to share an angel's smile?

IX.

'Twas then there lived a captive Hebrew pair.
  In woe the embraces of their youth had past,
And blest their paler years one daughter: fair
  She flourished, like a lonely rose, the last

And loveliest of her line. The tear of joy,
  The early love of song, the sigh that broke
From her young lip, the best beloved employ,
  What womanhood disclosed, in infancy bespoke

X.

A child of passion ; tenderest and best
  Of all that heart has inly loved and felt
Adorned the fair enclosure of her breast :
  Where passion is not found, no virtue ever dwelt.

XI.

Yet, not perverted, would my words imply
  The impulse given by heaven's great Artisan,
Alike to man and worm, mere spring, whereby
  The distant wheels of life, while time endures, roll on,

But the collective attributes that fill
  About the soul their all-important place ;
That feed her fires, empower her fainting will,
  And write the God on feeble mortal's face.

XII.

Yet anger or revenge, envy or hate,
  The damsel knew not : when her bosom burned,
And injury darkened the decrees of fate,
  She had more piteous sighed to see that pain returned.

XIII.

Or if perchance, though formed most just and pure,
  Amid their virtue's wild luxuriance hid,
Such germs all mortal bosoms must immure,
  Which sometimes show their poisonous heads unbid,—

If haply such the fair Judean finds,
  Self-knowledge wept the abasing truth to know;
And innate pride, that queen of noble minds,
  Crushed them indignant ere a bud could grow.

XIV.

And such, even now, in earliest youth are seen;
  But would they live, with armor more deform
Their breasts made soft by too much love must screen:
  "The bird that sweetest sings can least endure the
    storm."

XV.

And yet, despite of all, the starting tear,
  The melting tone, the blood suffusive, proved
The soul that in them spoke could spurn at fear
  Of death or danger; and, had those she loved

Required it at their need, she could have stood
  Unmoved as some fair-sculptured statue, while
The dome that guards it earth's convulsions rude
  Are shivering, meeting ruin with a smile.

XVI.

And this at intervals, in language bright,
  Told her blue eyes; though oft the tender lid
Drooped like a noonday lily, languid, white,
  And trembling, all save love and lustre, hid:

Then, as young Christian bard had sung, they seemed
  Like some Madonna in his soul, so sainted;
But, opening in their energy, they beamed
  As tasteful Grecians their Minerva painted:

While o'er her graceful shoulders' milky swell,
  Silky as those on little children seen,
Yet thick as Indian fleece, her ringlets fell,
  Nor owned Pactolus' sands a brighter sheen.

XVII.

And now, full near, the hour unwished for drew,
  When Sèphora had hoped to see her wed,
And, for 'twould else expire, impatient grew
  To renovate her race from beauteous Egla's bed.

XVIII.

None of their kindred lived to claim her hand;
  But stranger-youths had asked her of her sire
With gifts and promise fair. He could withstand
  All save her tears; and, hearkening her desire,

Still left her free: but soon her mother drew
  From her a vow, that, when the twentieth year
Its full fair finish o'er her beauty threw,
  If what her fancy fed on came not near,

She would entreat no more, but to the voice
  Of her light-giver hearken; and her life

And love, all yielding to that kindly choice,
  Would hush each idle wish, and learn to be a wife.

XIX.

Now oft it happed, when morning task was done,
  And lotted out for every household maid
Her light and pleasant toil, ere yet the sun
  Was high, fair Egla to a woody shade

Loved to retire. Acacias here inclined
  Their friendly heads, in thick profusion planted,
And with a thousand tendrils clasped and twined;
  And when, at fervid noon, all nature panted,

Inwoven with their boughs, a fragrant bower,
  Inviting rest, its mossy pillow flung;
And here the full cerulean passion-flower,
  Climbing among the leaves, its mystic symbols hung.

XX.

And though the sun had gained his utmost height,
  Just as he oped its vivid folds at dawn,
Looked still that tenderest, frailest child of light,
  By shepherds named "the glory of the morn."

XXI.

Sweet flower! thou'rt lovelier even than the rose:
  The rose is pleasure, — felt and known as such;
Soon past, but real; tasted while it glows:
  But thou, too bright and pure for mortal touch,

Art like those brilliant things we never taste
  Or see, unless with Fancy's lip and eye,
When, maddened by her mystic spells, we waste
  Life on a thought, and rob reality.

XXII.

Here, too, the lily raised its snow-white head;
  And myrtle-leaves, like friendship when sincere,
Most sweet when wounded, all around were spread;
And, though from noon's fierce heat the wild deer fled,
  A soft warm twilight reigned impervious here.

XXIII.

Tranquil and lone in such a light to be,
  How sweet to sense and soul! the form recline
Forgets it e'er felt pain; and Reverie,
  Sweet mother of the Muses, heart and soul are thine!

XXIV.

This calm retreat one summer day she sought,
  And sat to tune her lute: but all night long
Quiet had from her pillow flown; and thought,
  Feverish and tired, sent forth unseemly throng

Of boding images. She scarce could woo
  One song reluctant, ere, advancing quick
Through the fresh leaves, Sèphora's form she knew,
  And duteous rose to meet; but fainting, sick,

Her heart sank tremulously in her. Why
  Sought out at such an hour, it half divined;
And seated now beside, with downcast eye
  And throbbing pulse, she met the pressure kind,

And warmly given: while thus the matron, fair,
  Though marred by grief and time, with soothing word,
Solicitous, and gently serious air,
  The purpose why she hither came preferred.

XXV.

"Egla, my hopes thou knowest, though exprest
  Not oft, lest they should pain thee. I have dealt
Not rudely with thy fancies, yet my breast
  Retains the wish most vehemently felt.

"Know, I have marked that when the reason why
  Thou still wouldst live in virgin state thy sire
Has prest thee to impart, quick in thine eye
  Semblance of hope has played; fain to transpire,

"Words seemed to seek thy lip; but the bright rush
  Of heart-blood eloquent alone would tell,
In the warm language of a rebel blush,
  What thy less treacherous tongue had guarded well.

XXVI.

"Is the long frequent day spent lonely here?
  Or haply, rather, hath some stranger youth —

Then, Egla, see my heart!" — "O mother dear!
  Distrust my wisdom, but regard my truth.

XXVII.

"Long time ago, while yet a twelve-years' child,
  These shrubs and vines new-planted near this spot,
I sat me, tired with pleasant toil, and whiled
  Away the time with lute, and often thought

"Of the lost land thou lovest: every scene
  Which thou so oft, when I had climbed thy knee,
Wouldst sing of, weeping, through my mind had been
  In fair succession; when from yon old tree

"I heard a piteous moan. Wondering, I went
  And found an aged man: worn and oppressed
He seemed with toil, and said, in whispers faint,
  'O little maiden, how I am distressed!

"'I sink for very want. Give me, I pray,
  A drop of water and a cake: I die
Of thirst and hunger; yet my sorrowing way
  May tread once more, if thou my need supply.'

XXVIII.

"A long time missing from thy gentle arms,
  It chanced that day was sent me, in the shade,
New bread, a cake of figs, and wine of palms,
  Mingled with water, sweet with honey made.

XXIX.

'These brought I to him; tried to raise his head;
Held to his lip the cup; and, while he quaffed,
Upon my garment wiped the tears that sped
Adown his silvery beard, and mingled with the draught.

XXX.

"When, gaining sudden strength, he raised his hand,
And in this guise did bless me: 'Mayst thou be
A crown to him who weds thee! In a land
Far distant dwells a captive. Hearken me,

"'And choose thee now a bridegroom meet. To-day
O'er broad Euphrates' steepest banks a child
Fled from his youthful nurse's arms: in play
Elate he bent him o'er the brink, and smiled

"'To see their fears who followed him. But who
The keen, wild anguish of that scene can tell?
He bent him o'er the brink, and in their view,
But ah! too far beyond their aid, he fell.

XXXI.

"'They wailed; the long torn ringlets of their hair
Bestrewed the ambient gale; deep rolled the stream,
And swallowed the fair child: no succor there!
They, women,—whither look?—who to redeem

"'What the fierce waves were preying on? When, lo!
  Approached a stranger boy. Aside he flung,
Quick as a thought, his quiver and his bow;
  And, parted by his limbs, the sparkling billows sung.

XXXII.

"'They clung to an old palm and watched, nor breath
  Nor word dared utter; while the refluent blood
Left on each countenance the hue of death;
  Oped lip and far-strained eye spoke worse than death endured.

XXXIII.

"'But down the flood the dauntless boy appeared,
  Now rising, plunging, in the eddy whirled,
Mastering his course; but now a rock he neared,
  And, closing o'er his head, the dark, deep waters curled.

XXXIV.

"'Then Hope groaned forth her last, and to despair
  Yielded with shrieks; but ere the echo wild
Had ceased to thrill, restored to light and air,
  He climbs, he gains the rock, and holds alive the child!

XXXV.

"'Now mark what chanced! That infant was the son
  Of Babylonia's sovereign: soon was placed
Before his throne the youth who so had won
  From death the royal heir. A captive graced

"'All o'er with nature's gifts just dawning, brave,
And panting for renown, blushing and praised,
The stripling stood, and, closely pressed, would crave
Nought but a place mid warlike men: yet raised

"'To his full wish, the kingly presence leaving,
So light with airy hope, his graceful feet
Scarce touched the marble as he trod; while, heaving
With plans to please his sire, his heart more warmly beat.

XXXVI.

"'But, when his mother heard, she wept, and said,
"If he, our only child, be far away,
Or slain in war, how shall our years be stayed?
Friendless and old, where is the hand to lay

"'"Our white hairs in the earth?" So, when her fears
He saw would not be calmed, he did not part,
But lived in low estate to dry her tears,
And crushed the full ripe wish at his exulting heart.'

XXXVII.

"The old man ceased: ere I could speak, his face
Grew more than mortal fair; a mellow light,
Mantling around him, filled the shady place;
And, while I wondering stood, he vanished from my sight.

XXXVIII.

"This I had told; but shame withheld, and fear
Thou'dst deem some spirit guiled me, — disapprove, —
Perchance forbid my customed wandering here.
But, whenceso'er the vision, I have strove

"Still vainly to forget. I've heard thee mourn
Kindred afar, and captive: oh! my mother,
Should he, my heaven announced, exist, return,
And meet me here, lost! — wedded to another!"

XXXIX.

Then Sèphora answered, "In the city where
Our distant kindred dwell, blood has been shed.
Fond dreamer, had thy visioned love been there,
Ere now he's sleeping with the silent dead.

XL.

"Or doth he live, he knows not, would not know,
(Thralled, dead to thee, in some fair Syrian's arms,)
Who pines for him afar in fruitless woe,
And wastes upon a thought-love life and charms.

XLI.

"'Tis as a vine of Galilee should say,
'Culterer, I reck not thy support: I sigh
For a young palm-tree of Euphrates; nay,
Or let me him intwine, or in my blossom die.'

XLII.

"Thy heart is set on joys it ne'er can prove,
  And, panting ingrate, scorns the blessings given.
Hope not from dust-formed man a seraph's love,
  Or days on earth like to the days of heaven!

XLIII.

"But to my theme. Maiden, a lord for thee,
  And not of thee unworthy, lives and glows.
Nay, chase the dread that in thy looks I see,
  Nor make it taste of anguish to disclose

"What well might be delight. Rememberest thou,
  When to the altar by thy father reared,
As we went forth with sacrifice and vow,
  A victim-dove escaped, and there appeared

"A stranger? Quickly from his shrilly string
  He let an arrow glance; and to a tree
Nailed fast the little truant by the wing,
  And brought it, scarcely bleeding, back to thee.

XLIV.

"His voice, his mien, the lustre of his eye,
  And pretty deed he had done, were theme of praise,
Though blent with fear that stranger should espy
  Thy lonely haunts. When in the sunny rays

"He turned and went, with black locks clustering bright
Around his pillar neck, — ' 'Tis pity he,'
Thou saidst, 'in all the comeliness and might
Of perfect man, — 'tis pity he should be

"'But an idolater! How nobly sweet
He tempers pride with courtesy! A flower
Drops honey when he speaks. His sandalled feet
Are light as antelope. He stands a tower.'

XLV.

"That very stranger sought thy sire, and swore,
For the much love that day conceived for thee,
To be a false idolater no more.
'Tis Meles, late returned from embassy

"To distant courts, and loved by the young King
Of Media. Bethink thee, Egla: muse
Upon the good, union like this may bring
On thee and thine. Yet, if thy soul refuse,

"We will not press thee. Weep, if't be thy will,
Even on the breast that nourished thee, and ne'er
Distrest thee or compelled: this bosom still,
E'en shouldst thou blight its dearest hopes, will share,

"Nay, bear, thy pains. But sooner in the grave
'Twill quench my waning years, if reckless thou
Of what I not command, but only crave,
Canst see me pine, and disregard thy vow."

XLVI.

Then Egla: "Think not, kindest, I forget,
  Who have received such love, how much is due
From me to thee. The Mede I'll wed; but yet —
  Why will these tears gush forth? — thus — in thy presence too!"

XLVII.

Sèphora held her to her heart the while
  Grief had its way; then saw her gently laid,
And bade her, kissing her blue eyes, beguile
  Slumbering the fervid noon. Her leafy bed

Breathed forth o'erpowering sighs; increased the heat;
  Sleepless had been the night. Her weary sense
Could now no more. Lone in the still retreat,
  Wounding the flowers to sweetness more intense,

She sank. Thus kindly Nature lets our woe
  Swell till it bursts forth from the o'erfraught breast,
Then draws an opiate from the bitter flow,
  And lays her sorrowing child soft in the lap of rest.

XLVIII.

Now all the mortal maid lies indolent,
  Save one sweet cheek, — which the cool velvet turf
Had touched too rude, though all with blooms besprent, —
  One soft arm pillowed. Whiter than the surf

That foams against the sea-rock looked her neck
  By the dark, glossy, odorous shrubs relieved,

That, close inclining o'er her, seemed to reck
  What 'twas they canopied; and quickly heaved,

Beneath her robe's white folds and azure zone,
  Her heart yet incomposed; a fillet through
Peeped softly azure; while with tender moan,
  As if of bliss, Zephyr her ringlets blew

Sportive: about her neck their gold he twined;
  Kissed the soft violet on her temples warm,
And eyebrow just so dark might well define
  Its flexile arch, throne of expression's charm.

XLIX.

As the vexed Caspian, though its rage be past,
  And the blue smiling heavens swell o'er in peace,
Shook to the centre by the recent blast,
  Heaves on tumultuous still, and hath not power to cease;

So still each little pulse was seen to throb,
  Though passion and its pain were lulled to rest;
And ever and anon a piteous sob
  Shook the pure arch expansive o'er her breast.

L.

Save that, a perfect peace was sovereign there
  O'er fragrance, sound, and beauty; all was mute:
Only a dove bemoaned her absent fere,
  Or fainting breezes swept the slumberer's lute.

LI.

It chanced that day, lured by the verdure, came
  Zóphiël, a spirit sometimes ill, but, ere
He fell, a heavenly angel. The faint flame
  Of dying embers on an altar where

Zorah, fair Egla's sire, in secret bowed
  And sacrificed to the great unseen God,
While friendly shades the sacred rites enshroud,
  The spirit saw. His inmost soul was awed,

And he bethought him of the forfeit joys
  Once his in heaven. Deep in a darkling grot
He sat him down, the melancholy noise
  Of leaf and creeping vine accordant with his thought.

LII.

When fiercer spirits howled, he but complained
  Ere yet 'twas his to roam the pleasant earth.
His heaven-invented harp he still retained,
  Though tuned to bliss no more, and had its birth

Of him, beneath some black, infernal clift,
  The first drear song of woe; and torment wrung
The restless spirit less when he might lift
  His plaining voice, and frame the like as now he sung.

LIII.

"Woe to thee, wild ambition! I employ
  Despair's low notes thy dread effects to tell:

Born in high heaven, her peace thou couldst destroy;
And, but for thee, there had not been a hell!

"Through the celestial domes thy clarion pealed:
Angels, entranced, beneath thy banners ranged,
And straight were fiends; hurled from the shrinking field,
They waked in agony to wail the change.

"Darting through all her veins the subtle fire,
The world's fair mistress first inhaled thy breath;
To lot of higher beings learnt to aspire,
Dared to attempt, and doomed the world to death.

"The thousand wild desires that still torment
The fiercely struggling soul where peace once dwelt,
But perished; feverish hope; drear discontent,
Impoisoning all possest, — oh! I have felt

"As spirits feel: yet not for man we mourn:
Scarce o'er the silly bird in state were he
That builds his nest, loves, sings the morn's return,
And sleeps at evening. Save by aid of thee,

"Fame ne'er had roused, nor Song her records kept;
The gem, the ore, the marble breathing life,
The pencil's colors, all in earth had slept:
Now see them mark with death his victim's strife!

"Man found thee, Death: but Death and dull decay
Baffling, by aid of thee, his mastery proves;

By mighty works he swells his narrow day,
  And reigns for ages o'er the world he loves.

"Yet what the price? With stings that never cease
  Thou goad'st him on; and when too keen the smart,
His highest dole he'd barter but for peace,
  Food thou wilt have, or feast upon his heart."

LIV.

Thus Zóphiël still; though now the infernal crew
  Had gained by sin a privilege in the world,
Allayed their torments in the cool night-dew,
  And by the dim starlight again their wings unfurled.

LV.

And now, regretful of the joys his birth
  Had promised, deserts, mounts, and streams he crossed,
To find, amid the loveliest spots on earth,
  Faint semblance of the heaven he had lost.

LVI.

And oft, by unsuccessful searching pained,
  Weary he fainted through the toilsome hours;
And then his mystic nature he sustained
  On steam of sacrifices, breath of flowers.

LVII.

Sometimes he gave out oracles, amused
  With mortal folly; resting on the shrines;
Or, all in some fair sibyl's form infused,
  Spoke from her trembling lips, or traced her mystic lines.

LVIII.

And now he wanders on from glade to glade
 To where more precious shrubs diffuse their balms;
And gliding through the thickly-woven shade,
 Where the soft captive lay in all her charms,

He caught a glimpse. The colors in her face,
 Her bare white arms, her lips, her shining hair,
Burst on his view. He would have flown the place,
 Fearing some faithful angel rested there,

Who'd see him, 'reft of glory, lost to bliss,
 Wandering, and miserably panting, fain
To glean a joy e'en from a place like this:
 The thought of what he once had been was pain

Ineffable. But what assailed his ear?
 A sigh! Surprised, another glance he took;
Then doubting, fearing, softly coming near,
 He ventured to her side, and dared to look;

Whispering, "Yes, 'tis of earth! So, new-found life
 Refreshing, looked sweet Eve, with purpose fell,
When first Sin's sovereign gazed on her, and strife
 Had with his heart, that grieved with arts of hell,

"Stern as it was, to win her o'er to death.
 Most beautiful of all in earth or heaven!
Oh, could I quaff for aye that fragrant breath!
 Couldst thou, or being like to thee, be given

"To bloom forever for me thus! Still true
To one dear theme, my full soul, flowing o'er,
Would find no room for thought of what it knew,
Nor, picturing forfeit transport, curse me more.

LIX.

"But, oh, severest curse! I cannot be
In what I love blest e'en the little span
(With all a spirit's keen capacity
For bliss) permitted the poor insect, man.

LX.

"The few I've seen, and deemed of worth to win,
Like some sweet floweret, mildewed in my arms,
Withered to hideousness as foul as sin,
Grew fearful hags; and then, with potent charm

"Of muttered word and harmful drug, did learn
To force me to their will. Down the damp grave
Loathing I went at Endor, and uptorn
Brought back the dead, when tortured Saul did crave

"To view his lowering fate. Fair, ay, as this
Young slumberer, that dread witch, when, I arrayed
In lovely shape, to meet my guileful kiss,
She yielded first her lip. And thou, sweet maid! —
What is't I see? — a recent tear has strayed,
And left its stain upon her cheek of bliss.

LXI.

" She has fallen to sleep in grief; haply been chid,
  Or by rude mortal wronged. So let it prove
Meet for my purpose: 'mid these blossoms hid,
  I'll gaze, and, when she wakes, with all that love

"And art can lend come forth. He who would gain
  A fond, full heart, in love's soft surgery skilled,
Should seek it when 'tis sore; allay its pain
  With balm by pity pressed: 'tis all his own so healed!

LXII.

"She may be mine a little year, e'en fair
  And sweet as now. Oh respite! while possessed
I lose the dismal sense of my despair:
  But then — I will not think upon the rest!

LXIII.

"And wherefore grieve to cloud her little day
  Of fleeting life? What doom from power divine
I bear eternally! Pity! — away!
  Wake, pretty fly! and, while thou mayst, be mine,

"Though but an hour; so thou supply'st thy looms
  With shining silk, and in the cruel snare
Seest the fond bird intrapped, but for his plumes,
  To work thy robes, or twine amidst thy hair."

LXIV.

To whisper softly in her ear he bent,
  But draws him back restrained: a higher power,
That loved her, and would keep her innocent,
  Repelled his evil touch. And from her bower,

To lead the maid, Sèphora comes: the sprite,
  Half baffled, followed, hovering on unseen,
Till Meles, fair to see, and nobly dight,
  Received his pensive bride. Gentle of mien,

She meekly stood. He fastened round her arms
  Rings of refulgent ore; low and apart
Murmuring, "So, beauteous captive! shall thy charms
  For ever thrall and clasp thy captive's heart."

LXV.

The air's light touch seemed softer as she moved
  In languid resignation: his black eye
Spoke in quick glances how she was approved,
  Who shrank reluctant from its ardency.

LXVI.

'Twas sweet to look upon the goodly pair
  In their contrasted loveliness. Her height
Might almost vie with his: but heavenly fair,
  Of soft proportion, she, and sunny hair;
He cast in manliest mould, with ringlets murk as night.

LXVII.

And oft her drooping and resigned blue eye
  She'd wistful raise to read his radiant face:
But, then, why shrunk her heart?—a secret sigh
  Told her it most required what there it could not trace.

LXVIII.

Now fair had fallen the night. The damsel mused
  At her own window, in the pearly ray
Of the full moon: her thoughtful soul infused
  Thus in her words, left lone a while to pray:—

LXIX.

"What bliss for her who lives her little day
  In blest obedience, like to those divine,
Who to her loved, her earthly lord can say,
  'God is thy law, most just, and thou art mine!'

"To every blast she bends in beauty meek,—
  Let the storm beat, his arms her shelter kind,—
And feels no need to blanch her rosy cheek
  With thoughts befitting his superior mind.

"Who only sorrows when she sees him pained,
  Then knows to pluck away pain's keenest dart;
Or bid love catch it ere its goal be gained,
  And steal its venom ere it reach his heart.

"'Tis the soul's food: the fervid must adore.
  For this the heathen, unsufficed with thought,
Moulds him an idol of the glittering ore,
  And shrines his smiling goddess, marble-wrought.

"What bliss for her, even in this world of woe,
  O Sire who mak'st yon orb-strewn arch thy throne;
That sees thee in thy noblest work below
  Shine undefaced, adored, and all her own!

"This I had hoped; but hope too dear, too great,
  Go to thy grave! — I feel thee blasted now.
Give me fate's sovereign, well to bear the fate
  Thy pleasure sends: this, my sole prayer, allow!"

LXX.

Still fixed on heaven, her earnest eye, all dew,
  Seemed, as it sought amid the lamps of night
The God her soul addressed; but other view,
  Far different, sudden from that pensive plight

Recalled her. Quick as on primeval gloom
  Burst the new day-star when the Eternal bid,
Appeared, and glowing filled the dusky room,
  As 'twere a brilliant cloud. The form it hid

Modest emerged, as might a youth beseem, —
  Save a slight scarf, his beauty bare, and white
As cygnet's bosom on some silver stream;
  Or young Narcissus, when, to woo the light

Of its first morn, that floweret open springs:
   And near the maid he comes with timid gaze,
And gently fans her with his full-spread wings,
   Transparent as the cooling gush that plays

From ivory fount. Each bright prismatic tint
   Still vanishing, returning, blending, changing,
About their tender mystic texture glint
   Like colors o'er the full-blown bubble ranging

That pretty urchins launch upon the air,
   And laugh to see it vanish; yet, so bright,
More like — and even that were faint compare —
   As shaped from some new rainbow. Rosy light,

Like that which pagans say the dewy car
   Precedes of their Aurora, clipped him round,
Retiring as he moved; and evening's star
   Shamed not the diamond coronal that bound

His curly locks. And, still to teach his face
   Expression dear to her he wooed, he sought;
And in his hand he held a little vase
   Of virgin gold, in strange devices wrought.

LXXI.

Love-toned he spoke: "Fair sister, art thou here
   With pensive looks — so near thy bridal bed —
Fixed on the pale cold moon? Nay, do not fear:
   To do thee weal o'er mount and stream I've sped.

LXXII.

"Say, doth thy soul, in all its sweet excess,
  Rush to this bridegroom, smooth and falsehood-taught?
Ah, no! thou yield'st thee to a feared caress,
  And strugglest with a heart that owns him not.

LXXIII.

"Send back this Meles to Euphrates: there
  Is no reluctance. Withering by that stream,
Tell him there droops a flower that needs his care.
  But why, at such an hour, so base a theme?

LXXIV.

"I'll tell thee secrets of the nether earth
  And highest heaven! Or dost some service crave?
Declare thy bidding, best of mortal birth:
  I'll be thy wingèd messenger, thy slave!"

LXXV.

Then softly Egla: "Lovely being, tell,
  In pity to the grief thy lips betray
The knowledge of—say, with some kindly spell
  Dost come from heaven to charm my pains away?

LXXVI.

"Alas! what know'st thou of my plighted lord?
  If guilt pollute him,—as, unless mine ear
Deceive me in the purport of thy word,
  Thou mean'st to imply,—kind spirit, rest not here,

"But to my father hasten, and make known
The fearful truth. My doom is his command:
Writ in heaven's book, I guard the oath I've sworn,
Unless he will to blot it by thine hand."

LXXVII.

"Oaths sworn for Meles little need avail,"
Zóphiël replies: "Ere morn, if't be thy will,
To Lybian deserts he shall tell his tale:
I'll hurl him, at thy word, o'er forest, sea, and hill!

LXXVIII.

"But soothe thee, maiden! be thy soul at peace!
Mine be the care to hasten to thy sire,
And null thy vow. Let every terror cease:
Perfect success attends thy least desire."

LXXIX.

Then, lowly bending with seraphic grace,
The vase he proffered full; and not a gem
Drawn forth successive from its sparkling place
But put to shame the Persian diadem.

LXXX.

While he, "Nay, let me o'er thy white arms bind
These orient pearls, less smooth. Egla, for thee,
My thrilling substance pained by storm and wind,
I sought them in the caverns of the sea.

LXXXI.

" Look ! here's a ruby : drinking solar rays,
  I saw it redden on a mountain tip.
Now on thy snowy bosom let it blaze :
  'Twill blush still deeper to behold thy lip.

LXXXII.

" Here's for thy hair a garland : every flower
  That spreads its blossoms, watered by the tear
Of the sad slave in Babylonian bower,
  Might see its frail bright hues perpetuate here.

LXXXIII.

" For morn's light bell, this changeful amethyst ;
  A sapphire for the violet's tender blue ;
Large opals for the queen-rose zephyr-kist ;
  And here are emeralds of every hue,
For folded bud and leaflet, dropped with dew.

LXXXIV.

" And here's a diamond, culled from Indian mine
  To gift a haughty queen : it might not be :
I knew a worthier brow, sister divine,
  And brought the gem ; for well I deem for thee

" The ' arch-chymic sun ' in earth's dark bosom wrought
  To prison thus a ray, that when dull Night
Frowns o'er her realms, and Nature's all seems nought,
  She whom he grieves to leave may still behold his light."

LXXXV.

Thus spoke he on, while still the wondering maid
  Gazed as a youthful artist: rapturously
Each perfect, smooth, harmonious limb surveyed
  Insatiate still her beauty-loving eye.

LXXXVI.

For Zóphiël wore a mortal form; and blent
  In mortal form, when perfect, Nature shows
Her all that's fair enhanced. Fire, firmament,
  Ocean, earth, flowers, and gems, — all there disclose

Their charms epitomized: the heavenly power
  To lavish beauty, in this last work, crowned;
And Egla, formed of fibres such as dower
  Those who most feel, forgot all else around.

LXXXVII.

He saw, and, softening every wily word,
  Spoke in more melting music to her soul;
And o'er her sense, as when the fond night-bird
  Wooes the full rose, o'erpowering fragrance stole;

LXXXVIII.

Or when the lilies, sleepier perfume, move,
  Disturbed by two young sister-fawns, that play
Among their graceful stalks at morn, and love
  From their white cells to lap the dew away.

LXXXIX.

She strove to speak, but 'twas in murmurs low;
Her tender cheek the spirit's thrall expressing
In deeper hues of its carnation glow;
Her dewy eye her inmost soul confessing.

XC.

As the lithe reptile in some lonely grove,
With fixed bright eye, of fascinating flame,
Lures on by slow degrees the plaining dove,
So nearer, nearer still, the bride and spirit came.

XCI.

Success seemed his; but secret, in the height
Of exultation, as he braved the power
Which baffled him at morn, a subtle light
Shot from his eye, with guilt and treachery fraught.

XCII.

Nature upon her children oft bestows
The quick, untaught perception, and, while Art
O'ertasks himself with guile, loves to disclose
The dark thought in the eye, to warn the o'er-trusting heart.

XCIII.

Or haply 'twas some airy guardian foiled
The sprite. What mixed emotions shook his breast,
When her fair hand, ere he could clasp, recoiled!
The spell was broke; and doubts and terrors prest

Her sore. While Zóphiël: "Meles' step I hear!—
He's a betrayer!—wilt receive him still?"—
The rosy blood driven to her heart by fear,
She said, in accents faint but firm, "I will."

XCIV.

The spirit heard; and all again was dark,
Save as before the melancholy flame
Of the full moon, and faint, unfrequent spark
Which from the perfume's burning embers came,

XCV.

That stood in vases round the room disposed.
Shuddering and trembling to her couch she crept.
Soft oped the door, and quick again was closed;
And through the pale gray moonlight Meles stept.

XCVI.

But ere he yet with haste could throw aside
His broidered belt and sandals, dread to tell,
Eager he sprang; he sought to clasp his bride;
He stopt; a groan was heard; he gasped, and fell

XCVII.

Low by the couch of her who widowed lay,
Her ivory hands, convulsive, clasped in prayer,
But lacking power to move; and, when 'twas day,
A cold black corpse was all of Meles there!

CANTO SECOND.

DEATH OF ALTHEËTOR.

ARGUMENT.

Sardius, in his pavilion, alone with Altheëtor. —Description of the pavilion. — Sardius sends a detachment of his guards in search of Meles. — Egla and her parents are brought before the king to answer for the murder of Meles. — Egla relates the manner of Meles' death; is retained at the palace, and invited to banquet with Sardius and his princes. — Sardius determines to espouse Egla, but delays his purpose at the entreaty of Idaspes. — Egla is commanded, on pain of the death of her father, to receive as bridegroom whomever the king may appoint. — Alcestes, Ripheus, Philomars, and Rosanes, seek her chamber, and die in succession. — Sickness and death of Altheëtor. — Sorrow of Zóphiël. — Egla and her parents sent back to their home.

DEATH OF ALTHEËTOR.

I.

Soon over Meles' grave the wild flower dropt
  Its brimming dew; nor far where Tigris' spray
Leaps to the beam, in life's sweet blossom cropt,
  Four others, fair as he, were snatched from day.

Bridegrooms like him, they knew his fate, yet, bent
  On their desires, resolved that fate to brave:
So, in succession, each a victim went,
  Borne from the bridal chamber to the grave.

II.

Low liest thou, Meles! and 'tis mine to know,
  By light of song, the darkly hidden power
That closed thy bland but wily lip, and show,
  In flowing verse, what followed thy death-hour.

III.

Noon slept upon thy grave, and Media's king
  Had sat him down, from court and harem far,

With a young boy who knew to touch the string
  Of the sweet harp, and wage the ivory war

On painted field. The fainting breezes played
  Among the curling clusters of his hair;
Through myrtle blooms and berries, white and red,
  O'er the cool space of a pavilion, fair

As fond Ionian artist might devise:
  Twelve columns, ivory white, support a dome,
Painted to emulate the dark blue skies
  When seamen watch the stars, and sigh, and think of
    home;

IV.

And in the midst Night's goddess (to the sight
  More softly beauteous for a pictured moon
That mantles her in pale, mysterious light)
  Comes stealing to the arms of her Endymion.

V.

On six fair pedestals, ranged two by two
  Like Leda's sons, the smiling pillars stood;
As, each by either's side, they rose to view,
  Spotless from limpid bath in some deep, dusky wood,

Draining their dripping locks. In either space
  Between, three lattices, with blossoms bowered,
Alternate with three pictured scenes had place;
  And all who saw believed some god empowered

The gifted hand that spread their tints. In one,
  Far from the Grecian camp, his rage profound
Soothing, with lyre in hand, sat Thetis' son,
  Beside the ocean-wave that darkly dashed around.

VI.

Upon the next young Myrrha's form appears.
  Guilt, fear, repentance, blanch her cheek of love,
While, tender, beauteous, shuddering, drowned in tears,
  She flies the day, and hides in Saba's deepest grove.

VII.

A peerless third the bride of love displays,
  Psyche, with lamp in hand; blest, while unknown
The cause that gave her bliss; now daring rays
  The mystery pierce, and all her pleasures flown.

VIII.

Beneath that dome reclined the youthful king
  Upon a silver couch, and soothed to mood
As free and soft as perfumes from the wing
  Of bird that shook the jasmines as it wooed,

Its fitful song the mingling murmur meeting
  Of marble founts of many a fair device,
And bees that banquet, from the sun retreating,
  In every full, deep flower that crowns his paradise.

IX.

While gemmy diadem thrown down beside,
  And garment at the neck plucked open, proved
His unconstraint, and scorn of regal pride,
  When, thus apart retired, he sat with those he loved.

X.

One careless arm around the boy was flung,
  Not undeserving of that free caress,
But warm and true, and of a heart and tongue
  To heighten bliss, or mitigate distress.

XI.

Quick to perceive, in him no freedom rude
  Reproved full confidence: friendship, the meat
His soul had starved without, with gratitude
  Was ta'en; and her rich wine crowned high the banquet sweet.

What sire Altheëtor owned 'twere hard to trace:
  A beautiful Ionian was his mother.
Some found to Sardius semblance in his face,
  Who never better could have loved a brother.

XII.

But now the ivory battle at its close,
  "Go to thy harp,' said Sardius: "'twere severe
To keep thee longer thus." Then, as he rose,
  "Where's our ambassador? Call Meles here."

XIII.

Altheëtor said, "Alas! my prince, the chase
Detains him long; and yet from peril sure
'Tis deemed he fares: nay, those there are who trace
His absence to some sylvan paramour."

XIV.

"Let him be sought," said Sardius. No delay
Mocked that command; but vestige, glimpse, nor breath
Was gleaned, till sadly, on the seventh day,
A band returned with tidings of his death.

XV.

Sardius was sad upon his audience-seat.
Then spoke old Philomars: "Remember well,
O king! without the city, had retreat
Two of those captives of a race so fell,

"Thy father and my lord would rid the earth,
Root, branch, and bud, and gave the task to me;
But two escaped the sword, and so had birth
Another serpent. This, O prince! to thee

"Was told, and to complete the work I craved:
But thou didst check my zeal with angry mood,
And saidst, 'If any trembling wretch be saved,
Let him live on: there's been enough of blood.'

"We've traced Lord Meles to that serpent's den,
And seen him in the vile earth murdered lie:
Yet wherefore grieves the greatest king of men?
This only is the fruit of clemency."

XVI.

Then Sardius spoke (as on the earth he cast,
While grief gave anger place, his full dark eye): —
"Whoe'er has done this deed has done his last!
Soldier, priest, Jew, or Mede, by Belus he shall die."

XVII.

Then brought they Zorah in, misfortune's pride;
His venerable locks with age were white:
He cheered his trembling partner at his side,
Reposing on his God, befall him as it might.

XVIII.

Young Egla marked him stand so firm and pale;
Looked in her mother's face, — 'twas anguish there;
Then gently threw aside her azure veil,
And in an upward glance sent forth to heaven a prayer

XIX.

Then prostrate thus: "O monarch, seal my doom!
Thy sorrow for Lord Meles' death I know.
Take then thy victim, drag me to his tomb,
And to his manes let my life-blood flow!

XX.

"Oh! by the God who made yon glowing sun,
  And warmed cold dust to beauty with his breath,
By all the good that e'er was caused or done,
  Nor I nor mine have wrought thy subject's death.

XXI.

"Yet think not I would live. Alas! to me
  No warrior of my country e'er shall come;
And forth with dance and flowers and minstrelsy
  I go to bid no brother welcome home.

XXII.

"Sad from my birth, — nay, born upon that day
  When perished all my race, — my infant ears
Were opened first with groans; and the first ray
  I saw came dimly through my mother's tears.

"Pour forth my life, a guiltless offering
  Most freely given! But let me die alone!
Destroy not those who gave me birth! O king!
  I've blood enough: let it for all atone!"

XXIII.

She traced it on her hand, through the soft skin
  Meandering seen. Without, that hand was white
As drops for infant lip; the palm within
  Faintly carnationed, as of Amphitrit',

The fond Ionians fancied the pure shell
  Chosen by that loved goddess for a car,
While o'er her feet dissolving foam-wreaths fell
  In kisses: so they dreamed, in little bark afar.

XXIV.

Egla had ceased: her pure cheeks' heightened glow,
  Her white hands clasped, blue veil half fallen down,
Fair locks and gushing tears, stole o'er him so,
  That Sardius had not harmed her for his crown.

Yet, serious, thus fair justice' course pursued,
  As if to hide what look and tone revealed:—
"What lured a Median to thy solitude?
  How came his death? and who his corse concealed?"

XXV.

'Twas thus she told her tale: "A truant dove
  Had flown. I strayed a little from the track
That winds in mazes to my lonely grove,
  But heard a hunter's voice, and hastened back.

XXVI.

"Lord Meles saw; and with a slender dart
  Fastened the little flutterer to a tree
By the white wing, with such surpassing art,
  'Twas scarcely wounded when returned to me.

XXVII.

"Thankful I took; but, taught to be afraid
Of stranger's glance, retired: my mother sighed,
And trembling saw. Yet soon our dwelling's shade
The Median sought, and claimed me for a bride.

XXVIII.

"But when reluctant to my humble room
I had retired, was spread a fragrance there,
Like rose and lotus shaken in their bloom;
And something came and spoke, and looked so fair,

XXIX.

"It seemed all fresh from heaven. But soon the thought
Of things that tempt to sorcery in the night
Made me afraid. It fled, and Meles sought
His bridal bed: the moon was shining bright:

XXX.

"I saw his bracelets gleam, and knew him well;
But, ere he spoke, was breathed a sound so dread,
That fear enchained my senses like a spell;
And, when the morning came, my lord was dead.

XXXI.

"And then my mother, in her anxious care,
Concealed me in a cave, that long before
Saved her from massacre, and left me there
To live in darkness till the search was o'er

"Her fears foretold. So in that cavern's gloom
  Alone upon the damp bare rock I lay
Like a deserted corse; but that cold tomb
  Soon filled with rosy mists, like dawn of day,

"Which, half dispersing, showed the same fair thing
  I saw before; and with it came another,
More gentle than the first, — and helped it bring
  Fresh flowers and fruits, — in semblance like a brother.

XXXII.

"They spread upon the rock a flowery couch,
  And of a sparkling goblet bade me sip,
For that they saw me cold: I dared not touch,
  But, 'mid the sweet temptation, closed my lip;

"And from their grateful warmth and looks so fair
  I turned away, and shrank. Of their intent
I do not know to tell, or what they were,
  But feared and doubted both, and, when they went,

"Fled trembling to my home, content to meet
  The sternest death injustice might prepare,
Ere trust my weakness in that dark retreat
  To such strange peril as assailed me there."

XXXIII.

She ceased, and now, in palace bade to stay,
  Awaits the royal pleasure; but no more,

Though strictly watched and guarded all the day,
  To that stern warrior's threats was given o'er, —

Dark Philomars, strong in his country's cause;
  But harder than his battle-helm his heart:
Born while his father fought, and nursed in wars,
  Pillage and fire his sports, to kill his only art.

XXXIV.

And, when he sacked a city, he could tear
  The screaming infant from its mother's arms,
Dash it to earth, and, while 'twas weltering there,
  With demon grasp impress her shuddering charms;

Then, as she faints with shrieks and struggles vain,
  Coolly recall her with the ruffian blow;
And look, and pause, insatiate of her pain;
  Then gash her tender throat, and see the life-blood flow.

XXXV.

O Nature! can it be? The thought alone
  Chills the quick pulse: Belief retires afar;
Reason grows angry; Pity breathes a groan;
  And each distrusts the truth: yet "such things are."

Are! — nay, in this late age! God, canst thou view
  Thine image so debased? The bard in grief
Thinks o'er the creed of fiends; sees what men do;
  And, wondering, scarce rejects the wild belief.

XXXVI.

Night came ; and old Idaspes, all alone
With Sardius, had retired ; but why so late
He wakes, with his white hairs, may not be known ;
And still the captives tremble for their fate.

But, when the old man went, that gentle boy
Altheëtor sat by his loved master's couch ;
And fervent pleadings for their lives employ
His lips that else had sung. The while his touch

Thrilled o'er his lyre, gay Meles' early blight
Passed from the prince's thought : the transient gloom
Was to his soul just as some bird of night
Had flitted 'cross the moon, when, full and bright,
She o'er his garden shone in the sweet month of bloom.

XXXVII.

Of late his harem tired : if suns were there,
He did not burn, but sickened in their rays ;
And snow-white Egla, mild and chaste and fair,
Came o'er his fancy, as in sultry days

Soft clouds appear, when travellers bare the brow,
And, faint and panting, bless the timely shade,
And breathe the cool refreshment : so e'en now
Refreshed his languid soul the softly-imaged maid.

XXXVIII.

Or as some youth waked from the vine's excess,
Parched and impure, forgets the joys it gave,
And flies the fair Bacchante's wild caress
For some lone Naiad's grot, and cools him in the wave.

XXXIX.

Or as some graceful fawn, o'erspent with play,
Faints in the beam, and, where deep shades invite,
Flies, all impatient of the burning day,
And wooes the lily's shade to hide him from its light.

XL.

So felt the king: nor sleeping quite, nor waking,
As wildering o'er his lids the zephyrs sweep,
Whole beds of purple hyacinths forsaking;
And, when sweet revery gave place to sleep,

He dreamed of baths, or beds of flowers and dew,
Or sculptured marbles, as at Cnidos seen;
But still, with fair long locks, and veil of blue,
Another form would blend with every view,
With visionary grace and heavenly eye and mien.

XLI.

The smile of morning woke Idaspes' care;
And Egla, dubious if its light might bring
Or weal or woe to her, was bid prepare
To sit at evening banquet with the king.

XLII.

Then came an ancient dame, skilled in those arts
  Employed by Beauty's daughters to enchain
Or lightly touch the soft voluptuous hearts
  Of youths that seem, as they, of curl and eyebrow vain :

XLIII.

And, pouring perfumes in the bath, she told
  Wild tales of a Chaldean princess, loved
By the fair sprite Eroziel, who, of old,
  Taught all those trims to heighten beauty, proved

By Lydian, Median, Perse, and Greek ; with black
  To tip the eyelid ; stain the finger ; deck
The cheek with hues that languor bids it lack ;
  And how he taught to twine the arms and neck

With wreaths of gems, or made or found by him,
  Or his enamoured brothers, when they bore
Love for the like, and many a secret dim
  That nature would conceal, from charmed recesses tore.

XLIV.

This story o'er, the dainty maids were fain
  To take the white rose of her hand, and tip
Each taper finger with a ruddy stain
  To make it like the coral of her lip.

XLV.

But Egla this refused them, and forbore
The folded turban twined with many a string
Of gems; and, as in tender memory, wore
Her country's simpler garb to meet the youthful king.

XLVI.

Day o'er, the task was done; the melting hues
Of twilight gone, and reigned the evening gloom
Gently o'er fount and tower: she could refuse
No more, and, led by slaves, sought the fair banquet-
room;

XLVII.

With unassured yet graceful step advancing,
The light vermilion of her cheek more warm
For doubting modesty; while all were glancing
Over the strange attire that well became such form.

XLVIII.

To lend her space the admiring band gave way:
The sandals on her silvery feet were blue;
Of saffron tint her robe, as when young Day
Spreads softly o'er the heavens, and tints the trembling
dew.

XLIX.

Light was that robe as mist; and not a gem
Or ornament impedes its wavy fold,
Long and profuse; save that, above its hem,
'Twas broidered with pomegranate-wreath in gold;

L.

And, by a silken cincture broad and blue
  In shapely guise about the waist confined,
Blent with the curls, that, of a lighter hue,
  Half floated, waving in their length behind:
The other half, in braided tresses twined,
  Was decked with rose of pearls, and sapphires' azure
    too,

Arranged with curious skill to imitate
  The sweet acacia's blossoms, just as live
And droop those tender flowers in natural state;
  And so the trembling gems seemed sensitive,

And, pendent sometimes, touch her neck, and there
  Seem shrinking from its softness as alive;
And o'er her arms, flower-white and round and bare,
  Slight bandelets were twined of colors five,

Like little rainbows seemly on those arms:
  None of that court had seen the like before;
Soft, fragrant, bright,—so much like heaven her charms,
  It scarce could seem idolatry to adore.

LI.

He who beheld her hand forgot her face;
  Yet in that face was all beside forgot:
And he who, as she went, beheld her pace,
  And locks profuse, had said, "Nay, turn thee not."

LII.

Placed on a banquet-couch beside the king,
'Mid many a sparkling guest no eye forbore;
But, like their darts, the warrior-princes fling
Such looks as seemed to pierce, and scan her o'er and o'er:

Nor met alone the glare of lip and eye, —
Charms, but not rare: the gazer stern and cool,
Who sought but faults, nor fault or spot could spy:
In every limb, joint, vein, the maid was beautiful;

LIII.

Save that her lip, like some bud-bursting flower,
Just scorned the bounds of symmetry perchance,
But by its rashness gained an added power,
Heightening perfection to luxuriance.

LIV.

But that was only when she smiled, and when
Dissolved the intense expression of her eye;
And, had her spirit-love first seen her then,
He had not doubted her mortality.

LV.

And could she smile for that a stranger hung
O'er her fair form, and spoke to her of love?
Where is the youth who scorned a court, and sprung
Amid Euphrates' waves, as told her in her grove?

Haply she did, and for a while forgot
  Those dark acacias, where so oft was wept
Her lone, uncertain, visionary lot;
  Yet where an angel watched her as she slept.

LVI.

When light, love, music, beauty, all dispense
  Their wild commingling charms, who shall control
The gushing torrent of attracted sense,
  And keep the forms of memory and of soul?

LVII.

O theme of rapture, honored Constancy!
  Invoked, hoped, sworn, but rare! have we perchance
To thank the generous breast that nurtures thee
  For thy dear life, when saved? or fate or circumstance?

LVIII.

"Thy fragrant form, as the tall lily white,
  Looks full and soft, yet supple as the reed
Kissing its image in the fountain light,
  Or ostrich' wavy plume." So speaks the Mede,

While, bending o'er her banquet-couch, he breathes
  Her breath, whose fragrance wooes that near advance;
Plays with her silken tresses' wandering wreaths,
  And looks, and looks again with renovated glance.

LIX.

But, ever watchful, to his prince's side
  Came old Idaspes, — he alone might dare
To check the rising transport, ere its tide
  Arose too high to quell, — and thus expressed his care,

Whispering in murmurs first: "At last, O king!
  Thy subjects breathe; the cries of slaughter cease;
And happy laborers bless thee, as they bring
  Forth from thy smiling fields the fruits of peace.

"Their wounds just healing over, wouldst thou rush
  Upon thy doom and theirs? What bitter tears
Must flow if thou shouldst fall! what blood must gush!
  Wait till the cause of Meles' fate appears;

"And, ere this dangerous beauty be thy bride,
  Let him who loves thee best come forth and prove
The peril first." Alcestes rose beside,
  And said, "O prince! to prove my faith and love,

"I'll dare as many deaths as on the sod
  Without the falling rose of leaves has strown;
And, if bland Meles fell by rival god,
  So let me fall; and live the pride of Media's throne."

LX.

Egla, o'erwhelmed with shame, distaste, and fear,
  Could of remonstrance utter not a breath,
Ere fixed Idaspes' whisper met her ear, —
  "*One word impassive seals thy father's death.*"

LXI.

And, while Alcestes' bolder glances stray
  O'er the fair trembler to his monarch dear,
Not one distrustful whispering came to allay
  The sudden joy with slightest shade of fear.

A dark-haired priestess, well he knew, of late
  Had Meles loved; and, for the mystery
That hung so darkly o'er his early fate,
  Looked for no deadlier cause than wounded jealousy.

LXII.

And for the story of the cave, he deemed
  That lone, and in the dark, the frighted maid
Had gained a respite from her tears, and dreamed;
  Or haply framed the tale but to evade

Some feared result. But, be it as it might,
  The thoughtless king accedes; and, ere the day
Again had dawned, dead, ghastly to the sight,
  Before his bridal door the tall Alcestes lay.

LXIII.

So died the youth. But little might avail
His sacrifice; for Sardius, who forbore
His purpose but a while, contemned the tale,
And madly spoke thus, ere the day was o'er: —

LXIV.

"Ask of Alcestes' manes, did he die
By angry god or mortal's traitorous hand?
Whoe'er will draw to light this mystery,
Shall live the captain of my choicest band."

LXV.

That promise claimed Ripheus: he desired
No dearer boon; yet haply panted, less
By maddening thought of love and beauty fired
Than to a rival court to prove his fearlessness.

LXVI.

He had grasped the wily Parthian in the fight;
Leapt on the wounded tiger in the chase;
And oft his mother, vain in her delight,
Boasted she owed him to a god's embrace.

LXVII.

So he relied on that; and fickle chance
Conspired with the deceit, until his doom
Was rushed upon. But still his bold advance
Some caution guarded. To the fatal room

He came, and first explored with trusty blade;
  But, soon as he approached the fatal bride,
Opened the terrace-door, and, half in shade,
  A form, as of a mortal, seemed to glide.

LXVIII.

He flew to strike; but baffling still the blow,
  And still receding from the chamber far,
It lured him on; and in the morning low
  And bloody lay the form, which not a scar

Before had e'er defaced. Dismay profound
  Gave place to doubt; for, as by mortal hand
And mortal weapon made, the wound was found,
  And heard had been the clash that snapped his dinted
    brand.

LXIX.

Then came, with rage renewed, rough Philomars,
  (For gentle bridegroom's office most unmeet
Of all,) and craved, in guerdon of his scars,
  Permission to drag forth the deep deceit

He charged upon the daughter of the Jew,
  Whose life provoked his thirst; and pledged him, rife
With ancient hate, to bring her fraud to view,
  Or pay the bold aspersion with his life.

LXX.

Led from the bridal room a deep arcade,
 And paths of flowers; and fountains, often graced
With bathing beauty, now reflect the shade
 Of warriors tall and grim with helm and corselet braced.

LXXI.

They guard each pass, so that a bird in vain
 An outlet to his airy rounds might seek:
And Philomars stalked o'er the floor, with pain
 Stifling the rage which yet he dared not wreak;

And muttering 'twixt clinched teeth, "At last, young witch,
 Ends thy career!" then he, with careful touch
Of his proved sword, examined every niche;
 Then to the bride approached, and would have pierced her couch.

LXXII.

Not Eva, lovelier than the tints of air,
 Crouching amid the leaves lest heaven should see
That form, all panting 'neath her yellow hair,
 E'er looked more fair, or trembled more, than she.

LXXIII.

But the pale blaze of every fragrant lamp
 That moment died, as if a sudden gust
Of thick cold air had gushed from cavern damp;
 And, groping in the darkness, vainly curst

And struggled Philomars. 'Twas his last breath
That Egla heard, the suffocating noise
Of the one lengthened pang that gave him death:
She swooned upon her couch, but might not know the cause.

LXXIV.

The young Rosanes came at early morn
To view the corse, that lay in piteous case,
Grasping the sword its hand at eve had drawn,
The last fierce frown still stiff upon its face.

LXXV.

And thus the youth (in dress of horseman dight): —
"Art dead, old wolf? If ever, since his reign,
Pluto was grateful, take his thanks to-night;
For who has sent down more to people his domain?

LXXVI.

"But prithee, soldier, when the nether coasts
Receive thy soul, less grim and angry be,
Lest the fair sun be clouded o'er with ghosts
That rush again to earth to 'scape the sight of thee!"

LXXVII.

Rosanes of the painted eyebrow vain,
To gain report for wit and valor strove;
Rearing his Parthian courser on the plain,
And boasting, at the feast, of Naiad's love:

LXXVIII.

And round his neck an amulet he wore
  Of many a gem in mystic mazes tied;
And, mad for much applause, not long forbore
  To name his wishes for the dangerous bride.

LXXIX.

Enough to tell, he shared the common fate
  Of those whose rash adventurous zeal could dare
The spirit-guarded couch. But, oh! thy state,
  Altheëtor, generous boy! best claims the minstrel's
    care.

LXXX.

When Media's last king died a tumult rose,
  And all Idaspes' prudence scarce procured
To keep the youthful Sardius from his foes;
  And, ere his father's throne was yet secured,

Upon a terrace while Altheëtor hung
  About the prince, who carelessly carest,
A well-aimed arrow glanced: the stripling sprung,
  Stood like a shield, and let it pierce his breast.

LXXXI.

But sage Pithoës knew the healing good
  Of every herb: he plucked the dart away,
And stopped the rich effusion of his blood
  As at his monarch's feet the boy exulting lay;

LXXXII.

Drew forth from scrip an antidotal balm,
And, ere the venom through life's streams could creep,
Bestowed — for death's convulsions — dewy calm,
And steeped each throbbing vein in salutary sleep.

LXXXIII.

But now Altheëtor's sick. The kindly draught,
The bath of bruisèd herbs, were vainly tried;
While his young breath seemed as it fain would waft
His soul away, so piteously he sighed.

LXXXIV.

Above his couch were hung his sword and lyre,
His polished bow, and javelin often proved
In the far chase, where once in faith and fire
He fared beside to guard and watch the prince he loved.

LXXXV.

His fragrant locks, thrown backward from his brow,
Displayed its throbbing pulse: ah! how rebelled
That heart, the seat of truth! Beside him now
One languid hand the good Pithoës held,

LXXXVI.

And looked, and thought, and bent his brow in vain;
Then, in the sadness of his baffled skill,
Resigned the boy to fate; then thought again,
Was there no hidden cause for such consuming ill?

LXXXVII.

Still o'er the couch he casts his gentle eyes,
And brings fresh balm ; but all is unavailing.
Altheëtor faintly breathes his thanks, and sighs,
As if his guiltless life that moment were exhaling.

LXXXVIII.

'Twas long he had not spoke : now heaved his breast ;
And now, despite of shame, a tear was straying
From the closed, quivering lid. Some grief supprest,
Some secret care, upon his life was preying.

LXXXIX.

So came a glimpse across Pithoës' thought ;
And, in obedience to the doubt, he said, —
" 'Tis strange, Altheëtor, thou hast never aught
Asked or expressed of the fair captive maid ;

" For it was thou who forced the crowd to yield,
When she was rudely dragged, on audience-day,
And gently loosed from Philomars's shield
A lock of her fair hair he else had torn away.

XC.

" Sardius believed and loved her ; would have wed ;
But old Idaspes, doubtful 'twas some god,
That, amorous of her charms, laid Meles dead,
A while restrained the king, who saw, unawed,

"The gay Alcestes from her chamber fair
Thrown dead and black. Ripheus, too, lies low;
Old Philomars spoke his last curses there;
And young Rosanes ne'er his silver bow

"Shall draw again. And yet the king is fixed
In his resolve to wed: some power divine,
Envying our peace, impels; or she has mixed,
By magic skill, some philtre with his wine.

XCI.

"Or there's in her blue eye some wicked light
That steadily allures him to his doom.
She's bidden to the feast again to-night,
And good Idaspes' countenance in gloom

"Is fallen; in vain he strives; his silver hairs
Rise with the anguish at his heart's true core:
While the impatient, reckless Sardius swears
By Baal, whate'er betides, to wait but three days more.

XCII.

"Nor soldier, prince, or satrap, more appear
Vaunting their fealty firm with flattering breath;
But each speaks low, as if some god were near,
In silent anger singling him for death."

XCIII.

Now o'er Altheëtor's face what changes glistened
As ear and open lip drank every word !
He raised him from his couch, he looked, he listened,
Reviving, renovating, as he heard.

XCIV.

O'er cheek and brow a lively red was rushing,
While half he felt his dark eye could not tell ;
Then (spent the pang of hope) cold dews were gushing
From brow again turned pale. He drooped ; he fell

Faint on his pillow. Unsurprised and calm,
Soon to restore, the good Pithoës knew :
He saw what fever raged, and knew its balm ;
Spoke comfort to his charge ; and for a while withdrew.

XCV.

What in his breast revolved I cannot tell :
To seek Idaspes' aid his steps were bent ;
And when 'twas midnight, as by sudden spell
Restored, to bridal room Altheëtor went.

XCVI.

Touching his golden harp to prelude sweet,
Entered the youth so pensive, pale, and fair ;
Advanced respectful to the virgin's feet,
And, lowly bending down, made tuneful parlance there.

XCVII.

Like perfume soft his gentle accents rose,
  And sweetly thrilled the gilded roof along:
His warm devoted soul no terror knows,
  And truth and love lend fervor to his song.

XCVIII.

She hides her face upon her couch, that there
  She may not see him die. No groan! — she springs,
Frantic between a hope-beam and despair,
  And twines her long hair round him as he sings.

XCIX.

Then thus: " O being, who unseen but near
  Art hovering now, behold and pity me!
For love, hope, beauty, music, all that's dear,
  Look — look on me, and spare my agony!

C.

" Spirit! in mercy, make not me the cause,
  The hateful cause, of this kind being's death!
In pity kill me first! He lives! he draws —
  Thou wilt not blast? — he draws his harmless breath!"

CI.

Still lives Altheëtor; still unguarded strays
  One hand o'er his fallen lyre; but all his soul
Is lost, — given up: he fain would turn to gaze,
  But cannot turn, so twined. Now all that stole

Through every vein, and thrilled each separate nerve,
  Himself could not have told, all wound and clasped
In her white arms and hair. Ah! can they serve
  To save him? "What a sea of sweets!" he gasped;

But 'twas delight: sound, fragrance, all were breathing.
  Still swelled the transport: "Let me look — and thank,"
He sighs, celestial smiles his lip inwreathing:
  "I die — but ask no more," he said, and sank —

Still by her arms supported — lower — lower —
  As by soft sleep oppressed: so calm, so fair,
He rested on the purple tapestried floor,
  It seemed an angel lay reposing there.

CII.

Egla bent o'er him in amaze; a while
  Thanked God, the spirit, and her stars (so much
Like life his gently closing lids and smile);
  Then felt upon his heart. Ah! to that touch

Responds no quivering pulse: 'tis past. Then burst
  Her grief thus from her inmost heart that bleeds: —
"Nay, finish, fiend unpitying and accurst!
  Finish, and rid me too of life, and of thy deeds!"

CIII.

She hid her face in both her hands; and when,
  At length, looked up, a form was bending o'er
The good, the beauteous boy. With piteous ken
  It sought her eye, but still to speak forbore.

CIV.

A deep unutterable anguish kept
 The silence long; then from his inmost breast
The spirit spoke: "Oh! were I him so wept,
 Daughter of earth, I tell thee, I were blest.

CV.

"Couldst thou conceive but half the pain I bear,
 Or agent of what good I fain would be,
I had not — added to my deep despair
 And heavy curse — another curse from thee.

CVI.

"I've loved the youth since first to this vile court
 I followed thee from the deserted cave.
I saw him in thy arms, and did not hurt:
 What could I more? Alas! I could not save.

CVII.

"He died of love, — of the o'er-perfect joy
 Of being pitied, prayed for, prest by thee!
Oh! for the fate of that devoted boy
 I'd sell my birthright to eternity!

CVIII.

"I'm not the cause of this thy last distress.
 Nay! look upon thy spirit ere he flies!
Look on me once, and learn to hate me less,"
 He said; and tears fell fast from his immortal eyes.

CIX.

Her looks were on the corse. No more he said.
  Deeper the darkness grew; 'twas near the dawn:
And chilled and sorrowing through the air he sped,
  And in Hircania's deepest shades, ere morn,

Was hidden 'mid the leaves. Low moaned the blast,
  And chilly mists obscured the rising sun:
So bitter were his tears, that, where he past,
  Was blighted every flower they fell upon.

CX.

Wild was the place, but wilder his despair:
  Low shaggy rocks that o'er deep caverns scowl
Echo his groans: the tigress in her lair
  Starts at the sound, and answers with a growl.

CXI.

The day wore on: the tide of transport through,
  He listened to the forest's murmuring sound,
Until his grief alleviation drew
  From the according horrors that surround.

CXII.

And thus at length his plaintive lip expressed
  The mitigated pang: 'tis sometimes so
When grief meets genius in the mortal breast,
  And words most deeply sweet betray subsided woe.

CXIII.

"Thou'rt gone, Altheëtor: of thy gentle breath
  Guiltless am I, but bear the penalty!
Oh! is there one to whom thy early death
  Can cause the sorrow it has caused to me?

CXIV.

"Cold, cold, and hushed, is that fond, faithful breast:
  Oh! of the breath of God too much was there!
It swelled, aspired; it could not be comprest,
  But gained a bliss frail nature could not bear.

CXV.

"O good and true beyond thy mortal birth!
  What high-souled angel helped in forming thee?
Haply thou wert what I had been, if earth
  Had been the element composing me.

CXVI.

"Banished from heaven so long, what there transpires
  This weary exiled ear may rarely meet.
But it is whispered that the Unquelled desires
  Another Spirit for each forfeit seat

"Left vacant by our fall. That Spirit placed
  In mortal form must every trial bear
'Midst all that can pollute; and, if defaced
  But by one stain, it may not enter there.

CXVII.

"Though all the earth is winged, from bound to bound;
 Though heaven desires, and angels watch and pray,
To see their ranks with fair completion crowned,—
So few to bless their utmost search are found,
 That half in heaven have ceased to hope the day;
And pensive seraphs' sighs o'er heavenly harps resound.

CXVIII.

"And when, long wandering from his blissful height,
 One like to thee some quick-eyed Spirit views,
He springs to heaven, more radiant from delight,
 And heaven's blue domes ring loud with rapture at the news.

CXIX.

"Yet oft the being by all heaven beloved
 (So doubtful every good in world like this)
Some fiend corrupts ere ripe to be removed,
 And tears are seen in eyes made but to float in bliss.

CXX.

"Thou'lt take, perchance, Altheëtor, (who so pure
 That may if thou mayst not?) 'mid the bright throng,
My high, my forfeit place: love would secure
 Its prize, so killed thee ere below too long.

CXXI.

"Decay shall ne'er thy perfect form defile,
 Nor hungry flame consume. In dews I'll steep

Thy limbs, and thou shalt look upon the pile
As gentle as a maiden fallen asleep

"'Mid musings of ideal bliss, and making
Of her wild hopes, lit up by fancy's beam,
A fairer lover than may woo her waking,
Blest to her wish alone in soft ecstatic dream.

CXXII.

"And I will steal thee, when the perfumes rise
Around the cassia-wood in smoky wave:
I'll shroud thee in a mist from mortal eyes,
And gently lay thee in some sparry cave

"Of Paros; there seek out some kindly Gnome,
And see him ('mid his lamps of airy light),
By wondrous process done in earth's dark womb,
Change thee, smile, lip, hair, all, to marble pure and white.

CXXIII.

"O my loved Hyacinth! when as a god
I hurled the disk, and from thy hapless head
The pure sweet blood made flowers upon the sod,
'Twas thus I wept thee, — beautiful, but dead,

"Like all I've loved! — Oriel, false fiend, thy breath
Guided my weapon: come! most happy thou
If my pain please. I mourn another death:
Come with thy insect wings; I'll hear thy mockery now.

CXXIV.

"Thou didst not change his blood to purple flowers;
Thy poisonous breath can blight, but not create:
Thou canst but hovĕr o'er Phraërion's bowers,
And claim of men the honors of his state.

CXXV.

"Thou kill'st my Hyacinth; but yet a beam
Of comfort still was mine: I saw preserved
His beauty all entire, and gave a gleam
Of him to a young burning Greek. So served

"Thy crime a worthy cause: for, long inspired
With a consuming wish, that Grecian's heart,
Lost to repose, so caught what it desired;
And soon the chiselled stone glowed with a wondrous art."

CXXVI.

While thus the now half-solaced Zóphiël brings
Food to his soul, passed o'er his gloomier mood:
He shakes his ringlets, spreads his pinions, springs
From that rude seat, and leaves the mazy wood.

CXXVII.

That morn o'er Ecbatane rose pale and slow:
Thick lingering night-damps clog the morning's breath,
And veiled the sun that rose with bloody glow,
As if great Nature's heart bled for the recent death.

CXXVIII.

White-haired Idaspes from the fatal room
  Bade his own slaves love's loveliest victim bring, —
Fresh, fair, but cold, — and in that lurid gloom
  Set forth the funeral couch, and showed him to the king;

CXXIX.

And drew away the tunic from the scar
  Seen on his cold white breast. "And is it thou?"
He said: "when Treachery wings her darts afar,
  What faithful heart will be presented now?

CXXX.

"Alas! alas! that ever these old eyes
  Should see Altheëtor thus! Where is there one,
When lowly in the earth Idaspes lies,
  Will love and guard his prince as thou hast done?"

CXXXI.

Sardius believed he slept; but, undeceived,
  Soon as he found that faithful heart was cold,
He turned away his radiant brow, and grieved,
  And at that moment freely would have sold

CXXXII.

The diadem, that from his locks he tore,
  For that one life. Idaspes watched his mood,

And (ere the first fierce burst of grief was o'er,
While lost Altheëtor's every pulse) pursued

With guardian skill the kindly deep design:
He probed the king's light changeful heart, and gained
A promise that the maid of Palestine,
Until twelve moons had o'er his garden waned,

Should live in banishment from court. So, sent
To muse in peace upon her unknown love
(So long announced), dejected Egla went
With all her house, and seeks her own acacia-grove.

CUBA: PUEBLO NUEVO, June, 1827.

CANTO THIRD.

PALACE OF GNOMES.

ARGUMENT.

Midnight. — Zóphiël and Phraërion sit conversing together near a ruin on the banks of the Tigris. — Zóphiël laments his former crimes; speaks of a change in his designs; dwells on the purity of his love for Egla; and expresses a wish to preserve her life and beauty beyond the period allotted to mortals. — Phraërion is induced to lead the way to the palace of Tahathyam. — Palace and banquet of Gnomes. — Zóphiël, by force of entreaty and promise, obtains from Tahathyam a drop of the elixir of life.

PALACE OF GNOMES.

I.

'Tis now the hour of mirth, the hour of love,
  The hour of melancholy: Night, as vain
Of her full beauty, seems to pause above,
  That all may look upon her ere it wane.

II.

The heavenly angel watched his subject star,
  O'er all that's good and fair benignly smiling:
The sighs of wounded love he hears from far;
  Weeps that he cannot heal, and wafts a hope beguiling.

III.

The nether earth looks beauteous as a gem:
  High o'er her groves in floods of moonlight laving,
The towering palm displays his silver stem,
  The while his plumy leaves scarce in the breeze are
    waving.

IV.

The nightingale among his roses sleeps;
The soft-eyed doe in thicket deep is sleeping;
The dark-green myrrh her tears of fragrance weeps;
And every odorous spike in limpid dew is steeping.

V.

Proud prickly cerea, now thy blossom 'scapes
Its cell, brief cup of light, and seems to say, —
"I am not for gross mortals: blood of grapes,
And sleep, for them! — Come, Spirits, while ye may!"

VI.

A silent stream winds darkly through the shade,
And slowly gains the Tigris, where 'tis lost.
By a forgotten prince of old 'twas made,
And, in its course, full many a fragment crost

Of marble fairly carved; and by its side
Her golden dust the flaunting lotus threw
O'er her white sisters, throned upon the tide,
And queen of every flower that loves perpetual dew.

VII.

Gold-sprinkling lotus, theme of many a song
By slender Indian warbled to his fair!
Still tastes the stream thy rosy kiss, though long
Has been but dust the hand that placed thee there.

VIII.

The little temple where its relics rest
  Long since has fallen: its broken columns lie
Beneath the lucid wave, and give its breast
  A whitened glimmer as 'tis stealing by.

IX.

Here cerea, too, thy clasping mazes twine
  The only pillar time has left erect:
Thy serpent arms embrace it as 'twere thine,
  And roughly mock the beam it should reflect.

X.

An ancient prince, in happy madness blest,
  Was wont to wander to this spot, and deemed
A water-nymph came to him, and carest
  And loved him well: haply he only dreamed.

But on the spot a little dome arose,
  And flowers were set that still in wildness bloom;
And the cold ashes that were him repose
  Carefully shrined in this lone ivory tomb.

XI.

It is a place so strangely wild and sweet,
  That spirits love to come; and now upon
A moonlight fragment Zóphiël chose his seat,
  In converse close with soft Phraërion,

XII.

Who on the moss beside him lies reclining,
O'erstrewn with leaves from full-blown roses shaken
By nightingales, that, on their branches twining,
The livelong night to love and music waken.

XIII.

Phraërion, gentle Sprite! nor force nor fire
He had to wake in others doubt or fear:
He'd hear a tale of bliss, and not aspire
To taste himself; 'twas meet for his compeer.

XIV.

No soul-creative in this being born
Its restless, daring, fond aspirings hid:
Within the vortex of rebellion drawn,
He joined the shining ranks — as others did.

XV.

Success but little had advanced; defeat
He thought so little, scarce to him were worse;
And, as he'd held in heaven inferior seat,
Less was his bliss, and lighter was his curse.

XVI.

He formed no plans for happiness; content
To curl the tendril, fold the bud; his pain
So light, he scarcely felt his banishment.
Zóphiël, perchance, had held him in disdain;

But, formed for friendship, from his o'erfraught soul
'Twas such relief his burning thoughts to pour
In other ears, that oft the strong control
Of pride he felt them burst, and could restrain no more.

Zóphiël was soft, but yet all flame: by turns
Love, grief, remorse, shame, pity, jealousy,
Each boundless in his breast, impels or burns:
His joy was bliss, his pain was agony.

And mild Phraërion was of heaven; and *there*
Nothing imperfect in its kind can be:
There every form is fresh, soft, bright, and fair,
Yet differing each with that variety —

Not least of miracles — which *here* we trace,
And wonder, and admire the cause that formed
So like, and yet so different every face,
Though of the selfsame clay, by the same process warmed.

XVII.

"Order is heaven's first law." But that obeyed,
The planets fixed, the Eternal Mind, at leisure,
A vast profusion spread o'er all it made,
As if in endless change were found eternal pleasure.

XVIII.

Harmless Phraërion, formed to dwell on high,
Retained the looks that had been his above;

And his harmonious lip and sweet blue eye
 Soothed the fallen seraph's heart, and changed his scorn to love;

Who, when he saw him in some garden pleasant,
 Happy, because too little thought had he
To place in contrast past delight with present,
 Had given his soul of fire for that inanity.

XIX.

But, oh! in him the Eternal had infused
 The restless soul that doth itself devour,
Unless it can create; and fallen, misused,
 But forms the vast design to mourn the feeble power.

XX.

In plenitude of love, the Power benign
 Nearer itself some beings fain would lift,
To share its joys, assist its vast design
 With high intelligence: oh dangerous gift!

XXI.

Superior passion, knowledge, force, and fire
 The glorious creatures took; but each, the slave
Of his own strength, soon burnt with wild desire,
 And basely turned it 'gainst the hand that gave.

XXII.

But Zóphiël, fallen sufferer, now no more
Thought of the past: the aspiring voice was mute
That urged him on to meet his doom before,
And all dissolved to love each varied attribute.

XXIII.

"Come, my Phraërion, give me an embrace!"
He said. "I hope a respite of repose
Like that respiring from thy sunny face, —
Even the peace thy guileless bosom knows.

XXIV.

"Rememberest thou that cave of Tigris, where
We went with fruits and flowers and meteor light,
And the fair creature, on the damp rock, there
Shivering and trembling so? Ah! well she might!

"False were my words, infernal my intent,
Then, as I knelt before her feet, and sued;
Yet still she blooms, uninjured, innocent,
Though now for seven long months by Zóphiël watched and wooed!

XXV.

"Gentle Phraërion, 'tis for her I crave
Assistance: what I could have blighted *then*
'Tis *now* my only care to guard and save;
Companion, then, my airy flight again.

XXVI.

"Conduct me to those hoards of sweets and dews
Treasured — in haunts to all but thee unknown —
For favorite Sprites; teach me their power and use;
And whatso'er thou wilt of Zóphiël be it done!

XXVII.

"Throughout fair Ecbatane the deeds I've wrought
Have cast such dread, that of all Sardius' train
I doubt if there be one, from tent or court,
Who'll try what 'tis to thwart a Spirit's love again.

XXVIII.

"My Egla, left in her acacia-grove,
Has learnt to lay aside that piteous fear
That sorrowed thee; and I but live to prove
A love for her as harmless as sincere.

XXIX.

"Inspirer of the arts of Greece, I charm
Her ear with songs she never heard before;
And many an hour of thoughtfulness disarm
With stories culled from that vague, wondrous lore

"But seldom told to mortals, — arts on gems
Inscribed that still exist; but hidden so,
From fear of those who told, that diadems
Have passed from brows that vainly ached to know:

"Nor glimpse had mortal, save that those fair things,
Loved ages past like her I now adore,
Caught from their Angels some low whisperings,
Then told of them to such as dared not tell them more;

"But toiled in lonely nooks far from the eye
Of shuddering, longing men; then, buried deep,
Till distant ages bade their secrets lie,
In hopes that time might tell what their dread oaths must keep.

XXX.

"Egla looks on me doubtful, but amused;
Admires, but, trembling, dares not bid me stay:
Yet hour by hour her timid heart more used
Grows to my sight and words; and when a day

I leave her, for my needful cares, at leisure
To muse upon and feel her lonely state,
At my returning, though restrained her pleasure,
There needs no Spirit's eye to see she does not hate.

XXXI.

"Oft have I looked in mortal hearts to know
How Love, by slow advances, knows to twine
Each fibre with his wreaths, then overthrow
At once each stern resolve. The maiden's mine!

"Yet have I never pressed her ermine hand,
  Nor touched the living coral of her lip;
Though, listening to its tones, so sweet, so bland,
  I've thought — oh impious thought! — who formed might sip!

XXXII.

"Most impious thought! Soul, I would rein thee in,
  E'en as the quick-eyed Parthian quells his steeds;
But thou wilt start, and rise, and plunge in sin,
  Till gratitude weeps out, and wounded reason bleeds.

XXXIII.

"Soul, what a mystery thou art! not one
  Admires, or loves, or worships virtue, more
Than I; but passion hurls me on, till, torn
  By keen remorse, I cool, to curse me and deplore.

XXXIV.

"But to my theme. Now in the stilly night
  I hover o'er her fragrant couch, and sprinkle
Sweet dews about her, as she slumbers light, —
  Dews sought with toil, beneath the pale stars' twinkle,

"From plants of secret virtue. All for lust
  Too high and pure my bliss: her gentle breath
I hear, inhale, then weep (for, oh! she must;
  That form is mortal, and must sleep in death).

XXXV.

"And oft, when nature pants, and the thick air,
Charged with foul particles, weighs sluggish o'er,
I breathe them all: that deep disgust I bear,
To leave a fluid pure and sane for her.

XXXVI.

"How dear is this employ! how innocent!
My soul's wild elements forbear their strife;
While, on these harmless cares pleased and intent,
I hope to save her beauty and her life

"For many a rapturous year. But mortal ne'er
Shall hold her to his heart: to me confined,
Her soul must glow; nor ever shall she bear
That mortal fruit for which her form's designed.

XXXVII.

"No grosser blood, commingling with her own,
Shall ever make her mother. Oh! that mild,
Sad glance I love, that lip, that melting tone,
Shall ne'er be given to any mortal's child.

XXXVIII.

"But only for her Spirit shall she live,
Unsoiled by earth, fresh, chaste, and innocent;
And all a Spirit dares, or can, I'll give:
And sure I thus can make her far more blest,

"Framed as she is, than mortal love could do:
For more than mortal's to this creature given;
She's spirit more than half; her beauty's hue
Is of the sky, and speaks my native heaven.

XXXIX.

"But the night wanes: while all is bright above,"
He said,—and round Phraërion, nearer drawn,
One beauteous arm he flung,—"first to my love:
We'll see her safe; then to our task till dawn."

XL.

'Tis often thus with Spirits, when retired
Afar from haunts of men: so they delight
To move in their own beauteous forms attired;
Though like thin shades or air they mock dull mortals' sight.

XLI.

Well pleased Phraërion answered that embrace;
All balmy he with thousand breathing sweets
From thousand dewy flowers. "But to what place,"
He said, "will Zóphiël go? who danger greets

"As if 'twere peace. The Palace of the Gnome,
Tahathyam, for our purpose most were meet;
But then the wave so cold and fierce, the gloom,
The whirlpools, rocks that guard that deep retreat!

"Yet there are fountains which no sunny ray
  E'er danced upon ; and drops come there at last
Which for whole ages, filtering all the way,
  Through all the veins of earth in winding maze have
    passed.

XLII.

"These take from mortal beauty every stain,
And smooth the unseemly lines of age and pain, .
  With every wondrous efficacy rife :
Nay, once a Spirit whispered of a draught,
Of which a drop, by any mortal quaffed,
  Would save for terms of years his feeble flickering life."

XLIII.

"A Spirit told thee it would save from death
  The being who should taste that drop? Is't so?
O dear Phraërion ! for another breath
  We have not time ! Come, follow me : we'll go

"And take one look ; then guide me to the track
  Of the Gnome's palace. There is not a blast
To stir the sea-flower : we will go and back
  Ere morn. Nay, come : the night is wasting fast."

XLIV.

"My friend, O Zóphiël ! only once I went :
  Then, though bold Antreon bore me, such the pain,
I came back to the air so racked and spent,
  That for a whole sweet moon I had no joy again.

XLV.

" What sayst thou ? — back at morn ? The night, a day
 And half the night that follows it, alas !
Were time too little for that fearful way ;
 And then such depths, such caverns, we must pass ! "

XLVI.

" Nothing, beloved Phraërion ! I know how
 To brave such risks, and, first, the path will break,
As oft I've done in water-depths ; and thou
 Need'st only follow through the way I make."

XLVII.

The soft Flower-Spirit shuddered, looked on high,
 And from his bolder brother would have fled ;
But then the anger kindling in that eye
 He could not bear. So to fair Egla's bed
Followed, and looked ; then, shuddering all with dread,
To wondrous realms unknown to men he led ;

Continuing long in sunset course his flight,
 Until for flowery Sicily he bent ;
Then, where Italia smiled upon the night,
 Between their nearest shores chose midway his descent.

XLVIII.

The sea was calm, and the reflected moon
 Still trembled on its surface : not a breath
Curled the broad mirror. Night had past her noon.
 How soft the air ! how cold the depths beneath !

XLIX.

The Spirits hover o'er that surface smooth ;
  Zóphiël's white arm around Phraërion twined
In fond caress, his tender fears to soothe ;
  While either's nearer wing the other's crossed behind.

L.

Well pleased, Phraërion half forgot his dread,
  And first, with foot as white as lotus-leaf,
The sleepy surface of the waves essayed ;
  But then his smile of love gave place to drops of grief.

LI.

How could he for that fluid dense and chill
  Change the sweet floods of air they floated on?
E'en at a touch his shrinking fibres thrill ;
  But ardent Zóphiël, panting, hurries on,

And (catching his mild brother's tears, with lip
  That whispered courage 'twixt each glowing kiss)
Persuades to plunge : limbs, wings, and locks they dip :
  Whate'er the other's pains, the lover felt but bliss.

LII.

Quickly he draws Phraërion on, his toil
  Even lighter than he hoped : some power benign
Seems to restrain the surges, while they boil
  'Mid crags and caverns, as of his design

Respectful. That black, bitter element,
  As if obedient to his wish, gave way:
So, comforting Phraërion, on he went;
  And a high craggy arch they reach at dawn of day,

Upon the upper world; and forced them through
  That arch the thick, cold floods, with such a roar
That the bold Sprite receded, and would view
  The cave before he ventured to explore.

LIII.

Then, fearful lest his frighted guide might part,
  And not be missed, amid such strife and din,
He strained him closer to his burning heart,
  And, trusting to his strength, rushed fiercely in.

LIV.

On, on, for many a weary mile they fare,
  Till thinner grew the floods, long, dark, and dense,
From nearness to earth's core; and now a glare
  Of grateful light relieved their piercing sense;

As when, above, the sun his genial streams
  Of warmth and light darts mingling with the waves
Whole fathoms down; while, amorous of his beams,
  Each scaly monstrous thing leaps from its slimy caves.

LV.

And now Phraërion, with a tender cry, —
  Far sweeter than the land-bird's note, afar

Heard through the azure arches of the sky,
  By the long-baffled, storm-worn mariner, —

"Hold, Zóphiël! rest thee now: our task is done.
  Tahathyam's realms alone can give this light!
Oh! though 'tis not the life-awakening sun,
  How sweet to see it break upon such fearful night!"

LVI.

Clear grew the wave, and thin; a substance white
  The wide expanding cavern floors and flanks:
Could one have looked from high, how fair the sight!
  Like these the dolphin on Bahaman banks

Cleaves the warm fluid in his rainbow tints,
  While even his shadow on the sands below
Is seen, as through the waves he glides and glints
  Where lies the polished shell, and branching corals grow.

LVII.

No massive gate impedes; the waves in vain
  Might strive against the air to break or fall;
And, at the portal of that strange domain,
  A clear, bright curtain seemed, or crystal wall.

LVIII.

The Spirits pass its bounds, but would not far
  Tread the slant pavement, like unbidden guest;
The while, on either side, a bower of spar
  Gave invitation for a moment's rest.

LIX.

And, deep in either bower, a little throne
  Looked so fantastic, it were hard to know
If busy Nature fashioned it alone,
  Or found some curious artist here below.

LX.

Soon spoke Phraërion: "Come, Tahathyam, come!
  Thou knowest me well. I saw thee once to love,
And bring a guest to view thy sparkling dome,
  Who comes full fraught with tidings from above."

LXI.

Those gentle tones, angelically clear,
  Past from his lips, in mazy depths retreating
(As if that bower had been the cavern's ear)
  Full many a stadia far, and kept repeating

As through the perforated rock they pass,
  Echo to echo guiding them: their tone
(As just from the sweet Spirit's lip) at last
  Tahathyam heard, where on a glittering throne

He solitary sat. 'Twas many a year
  Ere such delightful, grateful sound had blest
His pleasured sense; and with a starting tear,
  Half joy, half grief, he rose to greet his guest:

LXII.

First sending through the rock an answering strain
To give both Spirits welcome where they wait,
And bid them haste; for he might strive in vain,
Half-mortal as he was, to reach that gate

For many a day. But in the bower they hear
His bidding, and, from cumbrous matter free,
Arose, and to his princely home came near
With such spiritual strange velocity,

They met him, just as by his palace-door
The Gnome appeared, with all his band, elate
In the display of his resplendent store
To such as knew his father's high estate.

LXIII.

His sire, a Seraph, framed to dwell above,
Had lightly left his pure and blissful home
To taste the blandishments of mortal love;
And from that lowly union sprang the Gnome,

Tahathyam, first of his compeers, and best:
He looked like heaven, fair semi-earthly thing!
The rest were born of many a maid carest
After his birth, and chose him for their king.

LXIV.

He sat upon a car (and the large pearl
Once cradled in it glimmered, now, without)
Bound midway on two serpents' backs, that curl
In silent swiftness as he glides about.

LXV.

A shell, 'twas first in liquid amber wet;
Then, ere the fragrant cement hardened round,
All o'er with large and precious stones 'twas set
By skilful Tsaveven, or made or found.

LXVI.

The reins seemed pliant crystal (but their strength
Had matched his earthly mother's silken band),
And, flecked with rubies, flowed in ample length
Like sparkles o'er Tahathyam's beauteous hand.

LXVII.

The reptiles, in their fearful beauty, drew,
As if from love, like steeds of Araby:
Like blood of lady's lip their scarlet hue;
Their scales so bright and sleek, 'twas pleasure but to
see.

LXVIII.

With open mouths, as proud to show the bit,
They raise their heads, and arch their necks (with eye
As bright as if with meteor fire 'twere lit),
And dart barbed tongues 'twixt fangs of ivory.

LXIX.

These, when the quick-advancing Sprites they saw
  Furl their swift wings, and tread with angel grace
The smooth fair pavement, checked their speed in awe,
  And glided far aside as if to give them space.

LXX.

The Gnome alighted with a pleasing pride,
  And, in like guise, to meet the strangers bent
His courteous steps; the while on either side
  Fierce Aishalat and Pshaämayim went;

LXXI.

Bright Ramaöur followed on, in order meet;
  Then Nahalcoul and Zotzaraven, best
Beloved, save Rouämasak of perfume sweet;
  Then Talhazak and Marmorak: the rest,

A crowd of various use and properties,
  Arranged to meet their monarch's wishes, vie
In seemly show to please the strangers' eyes,
  And show what could be wrought without or soil or sky.

LXXII.

And Zóphiël, though a Spirit, ne'er had seen
  The like before; and, for he had to ask
A boon almost as dear as heaven, his mien
  Was softness all. But 'twas a painful task

To his impatience thus the time to wait
  Due to such welcome, all his soul possest
With thoughts of Egla's lone, unguarded state;
  While still he smiled, restraining his request.

LXXIII.

But fond Phraërion looked on him, and knew
  How Zóphiël suffered in this smooth delay:
So toward the princely Gnome he gently drew
  To tell what lured them to these depths from day;

And said, "O king! this humble offering take:
  How hard the task to bring, I need not tell:
Receive the poor, poor gift, for friendship's sake!"
  Tahathyam took a yellow asphodel,

A deep-blue lotus, and a full moss-rose,
  And then spoke out, "My Talhazak, come hither;
Look at these flowers, cropt where the sunbeam glows;
  Crust them with diamond; never let them wither!"

LXXIV.

Then soon Phraërion: "Monarch, if 'tis truth
  Thou hast (and that 'tis false sweet powers forfend!)
A draught whose power perpetuates life and youth,
  Wilt thou bestow one drop upon my friend?"

LXXV.

Then Zóphiël could no more withhold, but knelt,
  And said, " O sovereign ! happier far than I !
Born as thou wert, and in earth's entrails pent,
  Though once I shared thy father's bliss on high.

LXXVI.

" One only draught ! and if its power I prove, —
  By thy sweet mother, to an Angel dear, —
Whate'er thou wilt, of all the world above,
  Down to these nether realms I'll bring thee every year.

LXXVII.

" Thy tributary slave, I'll scorn the pain,
  Though storms and rocks my feeling substance tear.
Tahathyam, let me not implore in vain :
  Give me the draught, and save me from despair."

LXXVIII.

Tahathyam paused, as if the bold request
  He liked not to refuse, nor wished to grant ;
Then, after much revolving in his breast, —
  " What of this cup can an Immortal want ?

LXXIX.

" My Angel sire for many a year endured
  The vilest toils, deep hidden in the ground,
To mix this drink ; nor was't at last procured
  Till all he feared had happed : death's sleep profound

"Seized my fair mother. I had shared her doom,
  Mortal, like her he held than heaven more dear;
But by his chemic arts he robbed the tomb,
  And fixed my solitary being here,

"As if to hide from the Life-giver's eye,
  Of his presumptuous task, untried before,
The prized success, bidding the secret lie
  Forever here. I never saw him more

"When this was done. Yet what avails to live,
  From age to age, thus hidden 'neath the wave?
Nor life nor being have I power *to give;*
  And here, alas! are no more lives to save.

LXXX.

"For my loved father's sight in vain I pine.
  Where is the bright Cephroniel? Spirit, tell
But how he fares, and what thou ask'st is thine."
  Fair hope from Zóphiël's look that moment fell.

LXXXI.

The anxious Gnome observed, and soon bethought
  How far his exile limited his will;
And, half divining why he so besought
  Gift worthless save to man, continued still

His speech: "Thou askest much: should I impart,
  Spirit, to thee, what my great father fain
Would hide from heaven, and what, with all his art,
  Even the second power desires in vain?

LXXXII.

"All long, but cannot touch: a sword of flame
 Guards the life-fruit once seen. Yet, Spirit, know
There is a service: do what I shall name,
 And let the danger threaten: I'll bestow.

LXXXIII.

"But first partake our humble banquet, spread
 Within these rude walls, and repose a while,"
He said; and to the sparry portal led
 And ushered his fair guests with hospitable smile.

LXXXIV.

High towered the palace and its massive pile,
 Made dubious if of nature or of art,
So wild and so uncouth; yet all the while
 Shaped to strange grace in every varying part.

LXXXV.

And groves adorned it, green in hue, and bright
 As icicles about a laurel-tree;
And danced about their twigs a wondrous light:
 Whence came that light so far beneath the sea?

LXXXVI.

Zóphiël looked up to know; and, to his view,
 Scarce seemed less vast than day's the vault that bent
In lofty arch, its soft, receding blue
 As of the sky, with tender cloudlets sprent;

LXXXVII.

And in the midst an orb looked as 'twere meant
  To shame the sun, it mimicked him so well.
But, ah ! no quickening, grateful warmth it sent :
  Cold as the rock beneath, the paly radiance fell.

LXXXVIII.

Within, from thousand lamps the lustre strays,
  Reflected back from gems about the wall ;
And from twelve dolphin shapes a fountain plays,
  Just in the centre of the spacious hall.

LXXXIX.

But whether, in the sunbeam formed to sport,
  These shapes once lived in suppleness and pride,
And then, to decorate this wondrous court,
  Were stolen from the waves, and petrified,

Or moulded by some imitative Gnome,
  And scaled all o'er with gems, they were but stone,
Casting their showers and rainbows 'neath the dome,
  To man or angel's eye might not be known.

XC.

No snowy fleece in these sad realms was found ;
  Nor silken ball, by maiden loved so well :
But, ranged in lightest garniture around,
  In seemly folds, a shining tapestry fell.

XCI.

And fibres of asbestos, bleached in fire,
  And all with pearls and sparkling gems o'erflecked,
Composed of that strange court the rich attire;
  And such the cold, fair form of sad Tahathyam decked.

XCII.

Of marble white the table they surround,
  And reddest coral decked each curious couch,
Which softly yielding to their forms was found,
  And of a surface smooth and wooing to the touch.

XCIII.

Of sunny gold and silver like the moon
  Here was no lack; but if the veins of earth,
Torn open by man's weaker race, so soon
  Supplied the alluring hoard, or here had birth,

That baffling, maddening, fascinating art,
  Half told by Sprite most mischievous, that he
Might laugh to see men toil, then not impart,
  The guests left uninquired: 'tis still a mystery.

XCIV.

Here were no flowers; but a sweet odor breathed
  Of amber pure: a glistening coronal
Of various-colored gems each brow inwreathed,
  In form of garland, for the festival.

XCV.

All that the shell contains most delicate,
Of vivid colors, ranged and dressed with care,
Was spread for food, and still was in the state
Of its first freshness: if such creatures rare
Among cold rocks, so far from upper air,
By force of art might live and propagate,
Or were in hoards preserved, the Muse cannot declare.

XCVI.

But here, so low from the life-wakening sun,
However humble, life was sought in vain;
But, when by chance or gift or peril won,
'Twas prized and guarded well in this domain.

XCVII.

Four dusky Spirits, by a secret art
Taught by a father thoughtful of his wants,
Tahathyam kept for menial toil apart;
But only deep in sea were their permitted haunts.

XCVIII.

The banquet-cups, of many a hue and shape,
Bossed o'er with gems, were beautiful to view;
But, for the madness of the vaunted grape,
Their only draught was a pure, limpid dew,

To Spirits sweet: but these half-mortal lips
  Longed for the streams that once on earth they quaffed;
And, half in shame, Tahathyam coldly sips,
  And craves excuses for the temperate draught.

XCIX.

"Man tastes," he said, "the grapes' sweet blood that streams
  To steep his heart when pained: when sorrowing, he
In wild delirium drowns the sense, and dreams
  Of bliss arise to cheat his misery."

C.

Nor with their dews were any mingling sweets
  Save those, to mortal lip, of poison fell:
No murmuring bee was heard in these retreats;
  The mineral clod alone supplied their hydromel.

CI.

The Spirits, while they sat in social guise,
  Pledging each goblet with an answering kiss,
Marked many a Gnome conceal his bursting sighs,
  And thought death happier than a life like this.

CII.

But they had music: at one ample side
  Of the vast area of that sparkling hall,
Fringed round with gems that all the rest outvied,
  In form of canopy was seen to fall

The stony tapestry, over what at first
  An altar to some deity appeared;
But it had cost full many a year to adjust
  The limpid crystal tubes that 'neath upreared

Their different lucid lengths; and so complete
  Their wondrous rangement, that a tuneful Gnome
Drew from them sounds more varied, clear, and sweet,
  Than ever yet had rung in any earthly dome,—

CIII.

Loud, shrilly, liquid, soft: at that quick touch
  Such modulation wooed his angel-ears,
That Zóphiël wondered, started from his couch,
  And thought upon the music of the spheres.

CIV.

Tahathyam marked; and, casting down the board
  A wistful glance to one who shared his cheer,
"My Ragasycheon," said he: at his word
  A Gnome who knew what strains his prince would
    hear

CV.

Arose, like youth's soft dawn in form and face,
  And than his many feres more lightly dressed;
Yet, unsurpassed in beauty and in grace,
  Silken-haired Ragasycheon soon expressed

The feelings rising at his master's heart,
  Choosing such tones as when the breezes sigh
Through some lone portico, or, far apart
  From ruder sounds of mirth, in the deep forest die.

CVI.

Preluding low in notes that faint and tremble,
  Swelling, awakening, dying, plaining deep;
While such sensations in the soul assemble
  As make it pleasure to the eyes to weep.

CVII.

Is there a heart that ever loved in vain,
  Though years have thrown their veil o'er all most dear,
That lives not each sensation o'er again
  In sympathy with sounds like those that mingle here?

CVIII.

Still the fair Gnome's light hands the chime prolong;
  And, while his utmost art the strain employs,
Cephroniel's softened son in gushing song
  Poured forth his sad, deep sense of long-departed joys.

CIX.

SONG.

O my Phronema! how thy yellow hair
  Was fragrant, when, by looks alone carest,
I felt it, wafted by the pitying air,
  Float o'er my lips, and touch my fervid breast!

How my least word lent color to thy cheek!
  And how thy gentle form would heave and swell,
As if the love thy heart contained would break
  That warm pure shrine where Nature bade it dwell!

We parted: years are past, and *thou* art dead:
  Never, Phronema, shall I see thee more!
One little ringlet of thy graceful head
  Lies next my heart: 'tis all I may adore.

Torn from thy sight, to save a life of gloom,
  Hopes unaccomplished, warmest wishes crost,
How can I longer bear my weary doom?
  Alas! what have I gained for all I lost?

CX.

The music ceased, and from Tahathyam passed
  The mournful ecstasy that lent it zest;
But tears adown his paly cheek fell fast,
  And sprinkled the asbestos o'er his breast.

CXI.

Then thus: "If but a being half so dear
  Could to these realms be brought, the slow distress
Of my long solitude were less severe,
  And I might learn to bear my weariness.

CXII.

"There's a nepenthic draught, which the warm breath
  Of mortals, when they quaff, keeps in suspense,

Giving the pale similitude of death
  While thus chained up the quick perceptive sense.

"Haply 'twere possible. — But to the shrine,
  Where like a god I guard Cephroniel's gift!"
Soon through the rock they wind: the draught divine
  Was hidden by a veil the king alone might lift.

CXIII.

Cephroniel's son, with half-averted face
  And faltering hand, that curtain drew, and showed,
Of solid diamond formed, a lucid vase;
  And warm within the pure elixir glowed,

CXIV.

Bright red, like flame and blood (could they so meet),
  Ascending, sparkling, dancing, whirling, ever
In quick perpetual movement; and of heat
So high, the rock was warm beneath their feet
  (Yet heat in its intenseness hurtful never),

Even to the entrance of the long arcade
  Which led to that deep shrine in the rock's breast,
As far as if the half-angel were afraid
  To know the secret he himself possessed.

CXV.

Tahathyam filled a slip of spar with dread,
  As if stood by and frowned some power divine;
Then trembling, as he turned to Zóphiël, said,
  "But for one service shalt thou call it thine.

CXVI.

" Bring me a wife, as I have named the way,
  (I will not risk destruction save for love !)
Fair-haired and beauteous like my mother : say,
  Plight me this pact ; so shalt thou bear above,

" For thine own purpose, what has here been kept
  Since bloomed the second age, to Angels dear.
Bursting from earth's dark womb, the fierce wave swept
  Off every form that lived and loved ; while here,
Deep hidden here, I still lived on and wept."

CXVII.

Then Zóphiël, pitying his emotion : " So
  I promise, — nay, unhappy prince, I swear
By what I dare not utter, — I will go
  And search, and one of all the loveliest bear

" Away, the while she sleeps, to be thy wife ;
  Give her nepenthic drink, and through the wave
Brave hell's worst pains to guard her gentle life.
  Monarch ! 'tis said : now give me what I crave !

CXVIII.

"Tahathyam Evanath, son of a sire
  Who knew how love burns in a breast divine,
If this thy gift sustain, one vital fire,
  Sigh not for things of earth ; for all earth's best are
      thine."

CXIX.

He took the spar: the high-wrought hopes of both
Forbade delay. So to the palace back
They came. Tahathyam faintly pressed, nor loath
Saw his fair guests depart to wend their watery track.

Cuba: Pueblo Nuevo, July, 1828.

CANTO FOURTH.

THE STORM.

ARGUMENT.

The gloom that precedes a tempest near Carthage. — Zóphiël and Phraërion returning from the palace of Gnomes. — Zóphiël loses the piece of spar which contains his invaluable elixir, and narrowly escapes being sucked down by a whirlpool. — Zóphiël and Phraërion emerge from the sea, and rest a moment in the deserts nearest Carthage: they attempt to pursue their course toward Media. — The storm increases. — Zóphiël meets a spirit who detains and reproaches him. — Phraërion seeks shelter. — Zóphiël and Phraërion return to Media.

THE STORM.

I.

Over that coast whither wronged Dido fled
  From brother's murderous hand low vapors brood,
But all is hushed; and reigns a calm as dread
  As that fell Roman's, who, like wolf pursued,

In after-times upon a fragment sate
  Of ruined Carthage, his fierce eye at rest;
While, hungry, cold, and spent, he mocked at fate,
  And fed on the revenge deep smouldering in his breast.

II.

But now that city's turrets frown on high;
  And from her distant streets is heard the shriek
Of frenzied mothers, uttered as they fly
  From where with children's blood their guilty altars
    reek.

III.

But far, far off, upon the sea's expanse,
  The very silence has a shriek of fear;

And, 'cross the sight, thick shadows seem to glance;
  And sounds like laughter ring, yet leave the ear

In racking doubt if it has heard such peal,
  Or if 'twas but affrighted fancy spoke:
Past that suspense, and, lesser pain to feel,
  As giant rends his chains, the bursting tempest woke.

IV.

Alas for the poor pilot at his prow,
  Far from the haven! Will his Neptune save?
The Muse no longer hears his frantic vow,
  But follows her fair Sprites still deep beneath the wave.

V.

Soon through the cavern the receding light
  Refused its beam. Zóphiël, with toil severe,
But bliss in view, through the thrice murky night
  Sped swiftly on. A treasure now more dear

He had to guard than boldest hope had dared
  To breathe for years: but rougher grew the way;
And soft Phraërion, shrinking back, and scared
  At every whirling depth, wept for his flowers and day,

Shivered, and pained, and shrieking, as the waves
  Wildly impel them 'gainst the jutting rocks:
Not all the care and strength of Zóphiël saves
  His tender guide from half the wildering shocks

He bore. The calm, which favored their descent,
  And bade them look upon their task as o'er,
Was past; and now the inmost earth seemed rent
  With such fierce storms as never raged before.

VI.

Of a long mortal life had the whole pain,
  Essenced in one consummate pang, been borne,
Known, and survived, it still would be in vain
  To try to paint the pains felt by these Sprites forlorn.

VII.

The Power that made, intending them for bliss,
  And gave their thrilling organs but to bless,
Had they been formed for such a world as this,
  Had kindly dulled their powers, and made their tortures less.

VIII.

The precious drop, closed in its hollow spar,
  Between his lips Zóphiël in triumph bore.
Now earth and sea seem shaken! Dashed afar,
  He feels it part; 'tis dropped; the waters roar.

IX.

He sees it in a sable vortex whirling
  Formed by a cavern vast, that, 'neath the sea,
Sucks the fierce torrent in; and, madly furling
  His wings, would plunge: one moment more, and he,
Sucked down, in earth's dark womb must wait eternity.

X.

" Pursue no farther ! — stop, alas ! for me,
  If not thyself ! " Phraërion's shrieks accost
Him thus : " Who, Zóphiël, shall protect for thee
  The maid thou lov'st? Hear ! stop ! or all are lost ! "

XI.

The verge, the verge, is near. Must such a state,
  Seraph, be thine? No ! sank the spar within ;
But the shrill warning reached him through the din
  Of waves. Back, back, he struggles, ere too late ;
  And the whole horror of the avoided fate
Shot through his soul. The wages of his sin
  He felt, for once, were light, and clasped his shrieking
      mate ;

XII.

Who thus entreats : " Up ! to earth's pleasant fields !
  O Zóphiël, all this torture's for thy pleasure ! "
Twined in his arms, the baffled Seraph yields,
  And flies the hungry depth that gorged his dearest
      treasure.

XIII.

What added torment — gained ; then snatched away, —
  Pressed to his heart, — and then to feel it riven
From heart and hand, while bearing it to-day
  With joy complete as if recalled to heaven !

XIV.

That which to own was perfect transport — lost!
  Yet still (to urge a dangerous course contending,
And the fierce passions which his bosom crost,
  For pity, or some other hope, suspending),

Resisting all, he forced a desperate way:
  His gentle fere, with plaints no longer vain,
Clung closer to his neck, nor ceased to pray
  To be restored to sun and flowers again.

XV.

Thus, all intwined, they rose again to air,
  Near Lybia's coast. Black clouds, in mass deform,
Were frowning; yet a moment's calm was there,
  As if had stopped to breathe a while the storm.

XVI.

Their white feet pressed the desert sod; they shook
  From their bright locks the briny drops: nor staid
Zóphiël on ills, present or past, to look;
  For, weary as he was, his lonely maid

Came to his ardent soul in all her charms:
  Unguarded she, what being might molest
Even now? His chilled and wounded substance warms
  But at the thought, the while he thus addrest

The shivering Sprite of flowers: "We must not stay:
All is but desolation here, and gloom.
Up! let us through the air, nor more delay.
Nay, droop not now: a little more essay,
I'll bear thee forward to thy bower of bloom,

"And on thy roses lay thee down to rest.
Come through the desert! banquet on thy store
Of dews and sweets! Come, warm thee at my breast!
On! through the air, nor think of danger more.

XVII.

"As grateful for the service thou hast done
I live, though lost the object of our task,
As if were still possessed the treasure won;
And all thou wouldst of Zóphiël freely ask.

XVIII.

"The Gnome, the secret path, the draught divine,
I know. Tahathyam sighs beneath the wave
For mortal bride: valor and skill are mine:
He may again bestow what once he gave."

XIX.

Thus Zóphiël, renovated, though the air
Was thick and dull, with just enough of hope
To save him from the stupor of despair,
Too much disdained the pains he felt to droop.

XX.

But soft Phraërion, smarting from his toil,
  To buffet not a tempest was in plight;
And Egla's lover saw him shrink, recoil,
  And beg some nearer shelter for the night:
  For now the tempest. bursting in its might,

Raged fiercely round, and made him fain to rest
  In cave or tomb. But Zóphiël gently caught him,
Sustained him firmly at his fearless breast,
  And 'twixt Euphrates and the Tigris brought him;

XXI.

Then paused a moment o'er a desert drear
  Until the thunder-clouds around him burst;
His flights renewed, and wished for Media near.
  But stronger grows the gale: what Sprites accurst

Ride on the tempest? Warring elements
  Might not alone such ardent course impede:
The wretched Spirit from his speed relents
  With sense like mortal bosom when they bleed.

XXII.

Loud and more loud the blast: in mingled gyre
  Flew leaves and stones, and with a deafening crash
Fell the uprooted trees: heaven seemed on fire, —
  Not, as 'tis wont, with intermitting flash,

But, like an ocean all of liquid flame,
  The whole broad arch gave one continuous glare;
While through the red light from their prowlings came
  The frighted beasts, and ran, but could not find a lair.

XXIII.

"Rest, Zóphiël, rest!" Phraërion cries. "The surge
  Was lesser pain: I cannot bear it more.
Beaten in seas so long, we but emerge
  To meet a fiercer conflict on the shore!"

XXIV.

Then Zóphiël: "There's a little grot on high;
  The wild doves nestle there; it is secure:
To Ecbatane but for an hour I'll fly,
  And come for thee at morn: no more endure.

XXV.

"Nay, wilt not leave me? Then I'll bear thee through
  As lately through the whirling floods I bore."
Still closer clinging, to his bosom grew
  The tender Sprite: "Then bear; I can no more,"

XXVI.

He said, and came a shock as if the earth
  Crashed 'gainst some other planet: shivered brands
Whirl round their heads; and (shame upon their birth!)
  Both Sprites lay mazed and prostrate on the sands.

XXVII.

The delicate Phraërion sought a cave
  Low-browed, and, crouching down 'mid trailing snakes
And slimy worms (things that would hide to save
  Their loathsome lives), hearkens the roar, and quakes.

XXVIII.

But Zóphiël, stung with shame, and in a mood
  Too fierce for fear, uprose; yet, ere for flight
Served his torn wings, a form before him stood,
  In gloomy majesty. Like starless night

A sable mantle fell in cloudy fold
  From its stupendous breast; and, as it trod,
The pale and lurid light at distance rolled
  Before its princely feet receding on the sod.

XXIX.

'Twas still as death, save that the thunder spoke
  In mutterings low and far: a look severe
Seemed as preluding speech; but Zóphiël broke
  The silence first: "Why, Spirit, art thou here?"

XXX.

It waved its hand, and instantaneous came
  A hissing bolt with new impetus back:
Darts round a group of verdant palms the flame,
  That, being pointed to them, blasted black.

XXXI.

"O source of all my guilt! at such an hour"
  (The mortal-lover said) "thine answer there
I need not read: too well I know thy power
  In all I've felt and feel. But has despair

"Or grief or torment e'er made Zóphiël bow?
  Declare me that, nor spend thine arts in vain
To torture more: if, like a miscreant, now
  I bend to thee, 'tis not for dread of pain;

"*That* I can bear. Yet bid thy legions cease
  Their strife. Oh! spare me this resistance rude
But for an hour; let me but on in peace;
  So shall I taste the joy of gratitude,

"Even to thee." — "The joy?" then first with scorn
  Replied that sombre being: "dream'st thou still
Of joy? — a thing accursed, demeaned, forlorn,
  As thou art? Is't for joy thou mock'st my will?

"Canst thou taste pleasure? banished, crushed, debased."
  "I can, betrayer! dost thou envy me?
But leave me to my wrongs, and I can taste
  Even yet of heaven, spite of my fall and thee.

XXXII.

"But that affects not thee: thine insults spare
  But for an hour; leave me to go at will

Only till morn, and I will back, and bear
  Whate'er thou wilt. What! dost obstruct me still?

"Thine armies dim, and shrouded in the storm,
  Then I must meet, and, weary thus and torn,
Essay the force of an immortal arm,
  Lone as I am, until another morn

"Shall shame both them and thee to thine abode.
  There, on the steam of human heart-blood, spilt
By priest or murderer, make repast; or brood
  Over the vile creations of thy guilt.

XXXIII.

"Waste thy life-giving power on reptiles foul,
  Slow, slimy worms, and poisonous snakes; then watch,
Like the poor brutes that here for hunger prowl,
  To mar the beauty that thou canst not match!"

XXXIV.

Thus he: the other folded o'er its breast
  Its arms, and stood as cold and firm the while
As if no passion stirred, save that expressed
  Its pale, pale lip a faint, ferocious smile.

XXXV.

While, blent with winds, ten thousand agents wage
  The strife anew; and Zóphiël, fain to fly,
But foiled, gave up to unavailing rage,
  And strove and toiled and strove, but could not mount
    on high.

XXXVI.

Then thus the torturer: "Hie thee to the bed
 Of her thou lov'st; pursue thy dear design;
Go dew the golden ringlets of her head!
 Thou wait'st not, sure, for any power of mine.

XXXVII.

"Yet better were the duties, Spirit dull,
 Of thine allegiance! Win her o'er to me,
Take all thou canst, — a pleasure brief but full,
 Vain dreamer, if *not mine,* she's lost to thee!"

XXXVIII.

"Wilt thou, then, hurt her? Why am I detained?
 O strength once serving 'gainst the powers above!
Where art thou now?" Thus Zóphiël; and he strained
 His wounded wings to mount, but could not move.

XXXIX.

Then thus the scorner: "Nay, be calm! I'll still
 The storm for thee: hear! it recedes; 'tis ended.
Yet, if thou dream'st success awaits thee, ill
 Dost thou conceive of boundless power offended.

XL.

"Zóphiël, bland Sprite, sublime Intelligence,
 Once chosen for my friend, and worthy me,
Not so wouldst thou have labored to be hence
 Had my emprise been crowned with victory.

XLI.

"When I was bright in heaven, thy seraph eyes
 Sought only mine. But he who every power
Beside, while hope allured him, could despise,
 Changed and forsook me in misfortune's hour."

XLII.

"Changed and forsook thee? This from thee to me,
 Once noble Spirit! Oh! had not too much
My o'er-fond heart adored thy fallacy,
 I had not now been here to bear thy keen reproach,"

XLIII.

Zóphiël replied. "Fallen, wretched, and debased,
 E'en to thy scornful words' extent, my doom
Too well I know, and for what cause displaced;
 But not from *thee* should the remembrance come!

XLIV.

"Forsook thee in misfortune? At thy side
 I closer fought as peril thickened round;
Watched o'er thee fallen: the light of heaven denied
 But proved my love more fervent and profound.

XLV.

"Prone as thou wert, had I been mortal-born,
 And owned as many lives as leaves there be,
From all Hyrcania by his tempest torn,
 I had lost them, one by one, and given the last for thee.

XLVI.

"Pain had a joy; for suffering could but wring
Love from my soul, to gild the murky air
Of our first rude retreat; while I, fond thing!
Still thought thee true, and smiled upon despair.

XLVII.

"Oh! had thy plighted pact of faith been kept,
Still unaccomplished were the curse of sin:
'Mid all the woes thy ruined followers wept,
Had friendship lingered, hell could not have been.

XLVIII.

"But when to make me thy first minister
Came the proposal, when thy purpose burst
Forth from thy heart's black den disclosed and bare,
Then first I felt alone, and knew myself accurst.

"Though the first seraph formed, how could I tell
The ways of guile? What marvel I believed,
When cold ambition mimicked love so well,
That half the sons of heaven looked on, deceived!

XLIX.

"Ambition thine; to me the Eternal gave
So much of love, his kind design was crost:
Held to thy heart, I thought thee good as brave,
Nor realized my guilt till all was lost.

L.

"Now, writhing at my utmost need, how vain
  Are Zóphiël's tears and prayers! Alas! heaven-born,
Of all heaven's virtues doth not one remain?
  Pity me once, and let me now be gone!"

LI.

"Go!" said the cold detainer with a smile
  That heightened cruelty; "yet know from me
Thy foolish hopes but lure thee on a while
  To wake thy sense to keener misery."

LII.

"O skilled in torment! spare me, spare me now!"
  Chilled by a dread foreboding, Zóphiël said;
"But little time doth waning night allow."
  He knelt; he wept: calm grew the winds; he fled.

LIII.

The clouds disperse. His heavenly voice he sent
  In whispers through the caves: Phraërion, there
In covert loathed, to that low music lent
  His soft, quick ear, and sprang to join his fere.

LIV.

Soon through the desert, on their airy way,
  Mantled in dewy mists, the Spirits prest,
And reached fair Media ere the twilight gray
  Recalled the rose's lover to his nest.

LV.

But on the Tigris' winding banks, though night
Still lingers round, two early mortals greet
The first faint gleam with prayer, and bathed and dight
As travellers came forth. The morn rose sweet,

And rushing by them, as the Spirits past,
In tinted vapors while the pale star sets:
The younger asked, "Whence are these odors cast
The breeze has waked from beds of violets?"

CUBA: PUEBLO NUEVO, August, 1828.

CANTO FIFTH.

ZAMEÏA.

ARGUMENT.

Morning. — Helon and Hariph travelling along the banks of the Tigris. — Helon is sorrowful in consequence of a dream of the preceding night; receives a box from Hariph. — Helon and Hariph see the princess Zameïa. — Neantes relates the story of Zameïa; her appearance in the temple of Mylitta; her love for Meles; the falsehood and dereliction of Meles; her sufferings; her escape from the garden of Imlec.

ZAMEÏA.

I.

How beauteous art thou, O thou morning Sun!
 The old man, feebly tottering forth, admires
As much thy beauty, now life's dream is done,
 As when he moved exulting in youth's fires.

II.

The infant strains his little arms to catch
 The rays that glance about his silken hair;
And Luxury hangs her amber lamps to match
 Thy face when turned away from bower and palace fair.

III.

Sweet to the lip the draught, the blushing fruit;
 Music and perfumes mingle with the soul:
How thrills the kiss, when feeling's voice is mute!
 And light and beauty's tints enhance the whole.

IV.

Yet each keen sense were dulness but for thee:
  Thy ray to joy, love, virtue, genius, warms.
Thou never weariest: no inconstancy
  But comes to pay new homage to thy charms.

V.

How many lips have sung thy praise! how long!
  Yet, when his slumbering harp he feels thee woo,
The pleasured bard pours forth another song,
  And finds in thee, like love, a theme forever new.

VI.

Thy dark-eyed daughters come in beauty forth
  In thy near realms; and, like their snow-wreaths fair,
The bright-haired youths and maidens of the North
  Smile in thy colors when thou art not there.

VII.

'Tis there thou bid'st a deeper ardor glow,
  And higher, purer reveries completest;
As drops that farthest from the ocean flow,
  Refining all the way, from springs the sweetest.

VIII.

Haply sometimes, spent with the sleepless night,
  Some wretch, impassioned, from sweet morning's breath
Turns his hot brow, and sickens at thy light;
  But Nature, ever kind, soon heals, or gives him death.

IX.

Fair Sun, no goodlier shape thy smiles this morn
  Caressed than Helon's, as he came from far,
A broidered scarf for girdle, closely drawn,
  And sandals on his feet, like Parthian messenger.

X.

The youth's brown ringlets in the loving beam
  Hung changeful, bright, and crisp: his neck, his bust,
Have thousand beauties all their own, and seem
  Not only moulded to proportion just,

But all his form, slightly attenuate,
  As best bespeaks activity, exprest
Something unseen; as if might emanate
  Excess of soul through the material breast,

That heaved and panted 'neath his garment blue
  (Which fell but to the knee); and, all about,
A warmth — a mystic charm — seemed breathing through
  Each viewless pore, and circling him without.

XI.

His youthful cheek was bronzed; and, though his eye
  Was of no vaunted hue, successive came
Of war and chase the quick variety;
  But oftener tenderness lent there her gentlest flame.

XII.

His sinewy arms were bare, and at his back
  A bow and quiver held their airy place:
Like some young hunter in the tiger's track
  He moved, with dart in hand, all symmetry and grace.

XIII.

But though (as rosy mists dispersed around,
  And birds sang sweet, and glistening meadows bloomed)
He met with passing joy the sight and sound,
  Yet Sadness o'er his face full soon her reign resumed.

XIV.

Nor this escaped an old man at his side,
  Whose looks told tales of many years: but fair
He was, and for a youth beseeming guide;
  Not Casius' peaks were whiter than his hair.

XV.

On hair or robe nor spot nor stain was seen,
  Though earth had been his bed, and dust his path:
Cool looked he in the sun, and pure and clean,
  As if in marble hall, and fresh from recent bath.

XVI.

And so he spoke: "Why, Helon, art thou thus
  Silent and sad? The desert way we've past
Has been a path of founts and flowers to us;
  Yet, at our wandering's close, I view thy brow o'er-
      cast."

XVII.

Then Helon said, "What cause for joy have I,
  Even were the uncertain dross we seek for found?
Who now regards my gentle mother's sigh
  While I am far? and what reward has crowned

"My father's worth and truth? Alas! our God,
  Who sits rejoicing in his mystery
And boundless power, I fear may not accord
  The least of his regards to them or me.

XVIII.

"Forsake but him, and palaces unfold
  Their hospitable gates to me and mine:
Now, for a beggar's hoard, a little gold,
  I go a wanderer forth, the last of all my line.

XIX.

"I gave up every youthful hope; nay, more,
  Would give up life as freely as a sigh:
For, if old Oran live, and should restore
  The treasure sought, our dwindled line must die.

XX.

"Why beats this heart? why is this arm so strong?
  Soon, to a little earth dissolved again,
Shall ever pen of scribe, or harper's song,
  Declare that one like Helon ere has been?

XXI.

"My sire and mother dead, around their tombs
I like a ghost must linger, loving nought:
Oh! if to this our God his faithful dooms,
Cast, cast me to the flames, and save me from the thought!"

XXII.

The old man looked upon him, marked his pain,
And love and pity mingled with that look;
For on his youthful brow was swoln the vein,
And like the fevered sick his pulses shook.

Yet on he spoke: "Still might I, warm with life,
Back to the queen of cities; take my place;
Choose from the bowers of Babylon a wife;
And bless my mother's eyes with a new blooming race,

"That else is lost. What though the fair I take
E'en from Mylitta's fanes? Women may be
Inthralled by love, and often will forsake
All other gods for love's idolatry."

XXIII.

The old man turned and uttered, "Do I hear
From *Helon* this? Some evil thing, some Sprite,
While darkness reigned, has whispered in thine ear,
And tempted thee, in visions of the night."

XXIV.

"Some *evil* thing!" returned the youth in mood
More vehement. "If evil things can give
Dreams such as mine, let me turn foe to good,
And make a God of *Evil* while I live!"

XXV.

"Make thee a God of Evil?" Hariph said:
"Too daring boy, the ambient viewless air
Teems with a race that hovers o'er thy head:
Woe to thy heart and thee if some find entrance there!

XXVI.

"From childhood nurtured 'neath the Baalic willow,
Where every breeze respires idolatry,
Thy soul, even as thy lip Euphrates' billow,
Has drank pollution, spite of Heaven and me."

XXVII.

"Pollution! Hariph, could such being beam"
(So Helon spoke) "as from a fearful death
I saved last night (ah! why was't but a dream?)
She would not be unworthy, though her breath

"Had been derived from Pagan sorcerer,
Priest of the Cnidian fanes, or priest of fire:
The signet of high heaven impressed on her
Gives to oblivion these, and stamps her heavenly sire!"

XXVIII.

The old man turned, and cast upon the boy
(Who for his fervor spoke in impious guise)
An anxious glance; but yet a secret joy,
The while he thus reproved, seemed hidden in his eyes.

XXIX.

"Thy doubts and words are guilty! 'Tis not given
To son of mortal (though he even may be
O'erwatched and well beloved by those of heaven)
To know what beings sway his destiny.

XXX.

"Thy dream was good; but, lest thyself undo
All that is done, I tell thee, youth, beware!
Curb thine impatience; keep thy God in view,
Nor murmur at the cup his wisdom may prepare.

"Virtue! how many as a lowly thing,
Born of weak folly, scorn thee! but thy name
Alone they know: upon thy soaring wing
They'd fear to mount; nor could thy sacred flame

"Burn in their baser hearts: the biting thorn,
The flinty crag, flowers hiding, strew thy field;
Yet blest is he whose daring bides the scorn
Of the frail easy herd, and buckles on thy shield.

"Who says thy ways are bliss, trolls but a lay
  To lure the infant: if thy paths to view
Were always pleasant, Crime's worst sons would lay
  Their daggers at thy feet, and *from mere sloth* pursue.

XXXI.

"Nor deed nor prayer nor suffering of the just
  Is ever lost" (he said; his clear eye flashed):
"Tempt not the powers that love thee, more!" Then first
  The youth felt awe, and dropped his lids abashed.

XXXII.

Still Hariph spoke: "If ever thou shouldst live
  To be in danger from a potent Sprite,
Recall me to thy mind; take what I give,
  And burn whate'er it holds, with perfume, in his sight."

XXXIII.

Helon received a little box composed
  Of carneol; and the sunbeams, as they rushed
Through the transparent hollow gem, disclosed
  What seemed a serpent's heart, but dried and crushed.

XXXIV.

Then bent they near a thicket, side by side,
  Their friendly way, nor more in words exprest;
But often Helon looked upon his guide,
  And seemed communing with his inmost breast.

XXXV.

Warm grew the day; and now, as if to mock
  Their sight, with sudden wind the river swept.
They turn a mossy, dark, projecting rock,
  And start; for 'neath its crags a woman slept,

Pallid and worn, but beautiful and young,
  Though marked her charms by wildest passion's trace:
Her long round arms, over a fragment flung,
  From pillow all too rude protect a face

Whose dark and high-arched brows gave to the thought
  To deem what radiance once they towered above;
But all its proudly beauteous outline taught
  That anger there had shared the throne of love.

XXXVI.

Rich are her robes, but torn and soiled; and gleams
  Above her belt a dagger set with gems:
Her long black hair, 'scaped from its braiding, streams,
  Black as a serpent, to her garments' hems.

XXXVII.

Black as a serpent. — Daughters of the woods,
  You see him 'mid Mechaceba's roses, while
Your light canoes upon the vernal floods
  Are thrown to bear you to some floating isle,

Where sleeping bisons sail upon the tide:
There, while through golden-blossomed nenuphar
Your arrows pierce some tall flamingo's side,
He rears his white-ringed neck, and watches you from far.

XXXVIII.

Her sandalled feet were scarred, and drops of blood
Still rested fresh on them, by tooth of thorn
Expressed; and, let day's eye look where it would,
'Twere hard to find such beauty so forlorn.

XXXIX.

Near on the moss lay one who seemed her guide;
A mule among the herbs his pittance took;
A little slave of Ethiope, at her side,
Sat watching o'er them all with many a sorrowing look.

XL.

Helon drew back, but only half suppressed
The cry surprise propelled. "What strange mischance
Brings to the desert these?" While so addressed
Hariph, the one on earth awoke beneath their glance,

And laid his finger on his lip in fear,
And on the sleeper gazed: she did not stir.
Then, wiping from his sunken eye a tear,
He fell before their feet, a suppliant for her.

XLI.

Then Helon thus: "Distrust us not, but tell
  Why thou art here, and who is that soft dame?
Thyself, thine accent, and her garb, speak well
  That from the City of the Dove ye came."

XLII.

"I'm one," he said, "by cruel man designed
  The doubtful faith, in absence, to protect
Of hearts as wayward as the desert wind;
  And which, despite of all, love only can subject.

XLIII.

"To care of women nurtured from a boy,
  Stranger, in me a suffering wretch you see
Ripened to age, but in that soft employ
  A princess' only guard, but frail and weak as she.

XLIV.

"Our silken limbs, by biting brambles torn,
  Have felt the noontide heat and drenching rain;
And that bright maid, for love and pleasure born,
  Breathes to the desert-blast her burning sighs in vain.

XLV.

"Yet have we lived adorers of that Power
  Which to the death-reaped world a race supplies
  As numerous as the stars of midnight skies,
Or desert sands, or dust from every flower
  That blossoms by the stream that flowed from Paradise.

XLVI.

" Divine Mylitta, child of light, and *that*
Which from dark nothing formed the teeming earth;
Of *that* which on the circling waters sat,
And warmed, and charmed, and ranged, till Nature sprang to birth!—

XLVII.

" Divine Mylitta, kindler of the flames
That light life's lamp! in duteousness to thee
I brought this gem, this sun of Syrian dames;
But, now thy slave and Love's, thou mock'st her misery."

XLVIII.

Then Helon spoke: " Has any wretch, more fell
Than he who first his hurtful arts essayed
On her of Paradise, done this? Nay, tell
Thy tale; and take, if we can lend thee, aid."

XLIX.

" Then listen, stranger; but for Belus' sake
Let her sleep on who hath such need of rest,"
Zameïa's guardian said; " for, when awake,
The flames of Tartarus are in her breast.

L.

" She sat and raved last eve in the pale light
Till the fair moon she looked on seemed to shrink
From her distress: fearing some spell or blight,
I drew her to this grot, and drugged her drink."

LI.

Then softly near to her wild couch he drew,
  Twining the tendrils o'er her, as he can,
To save from sun as they had saved from dew;
  Then sat him on the rock, and thus his story ran: —

LII.

"The warrior Imlec by Euphrates' side
  Received his birth: there haply still he thrives;
And, when he took Zameïa for a bride,
  His beard was white, and he had many wives.

LIII.

"Now, when I tell thee her inconstancy,
  Let thoughts of pity mingle with the blame
'Tis just to cast upon adultery,
  And scorn and coldness to the nuptial flame.

LIV.

"There's oft which, were it known, might wash away
  Full half the stain of guilt: fame will not heed
The train of lesser truths, but drags to day,
  And shows the shuddering world, all bare and black, the deed.

LV.

"There were who said that Imlec's life was vile,
  Even when possessed of all her blooming charms:
How could she else than loathe, who knew the while
  He came exhausted from an Ethiop's arms?

LVI.

" Whate'er the cause, she ever would rebel:
Yet, when increased, her loathing pleased him best;
And, for caprice or love, it so befell,
He built for her, apart from all the rest,

LVII.

" A precious palace, and a garden fair,
And gave to me the charge, from every ill
To keep and guard her well; nor ever dare,
Unless it wronged his love, to cross in aught her will.

LVIII.

" So she had founts and birds, and gems and gold;
And care of these and her was given to me;
And Imlec (in his youth a warrior bold)
Beyond the Indus went on embassy.

LIX.

" Do all I could, she sullen grew, and sad,
And very oft the public streets would see,
And oft (alas! what days of fear I had!)
Her deep disgust for Imlec spoke to me.

LX.

" I knew his jealousy, and was afraid;
For, if there fell upon her fame a breath
(While treating with the Indian king he staid),
I had been charged to answer it with death.

LXI.

"What could I? Bland Mylitta, patroness
Of rich Assyria and her glowing fair,
I sought; but no propitious sign might bless
The milk-white doves and flowers of beauty rare

LXII.

"I daily brought: the goddess scorned my pains,
And turned from all my gifts her heavenly eyes;
For yet the princess never, at her fanes,
Of her young charms had made the sacrifice

"Required of every Babylonian dame,
Whoe'er her lord or sire. This was my care;
And, when the opening of the roses came,
With many a votive wreath I led Zameïa there.

LXIII.

"Oh! it was sweet to see in marble pure
The semblance of the goddess while she smiled,
As, in her own eternal power secure,
She watched the movements of her light-winged child.

LXIV.

"Nor e'er had icy marble la'en such charm;
Save that the deity once, in a dream,
Came to her sculptor all alive and warm,
And gave him power to catch each glow and gleam.

LXV.

"And seemed her lip to deeper pleasure changing,
While to her temple rushed the adoring crowd,
And groups, almost as fair as she, arranging
Their offerings at her feet, in soft submission bowed.

LXVI.

"The tender breeze, that, sighing all about,
Their musky locks with roses woven greets,—
Now whispering through the myrtle-groves without,
Now fainting with variety of sweets.

LXVII.

"A fairer scene warm Syria never shall
Behold, nor ever had beheld before.
Full many a stranger thronged the festival;
And here, whate'er their god, how could they but adore?

LXVIII.

"But of the gentle votarists, some in tears,
And lips amidst their adoration quivering,
While a soft horror in their look appears,
Do all they could, with fear and doubt were shivering.

LXIX.

"Some, formed for faith and tenderest constancy,
But to avert Heaven's anger sought the place,
And breathe for absent lord the blameless sigh,
And shudder at the stranger's rude embrace.

LXX.

" Some, in whose panting hearts the natural void
Had never yet been filled, all in a glow
Of dubious hope, their fervid thoughts employed
In picturing all they wished a moment might bestow.

LXXI.

" Full in the midst, and taller than the rest,
Zameïa stood distinct; and not a sigh
Disturbed the gem that sparkled on her breast:
Her oval cheek was heightened to a dye

" That shamed the mellow vermeil of the wreath
Which in her jetty locks became her well,
And mingled fragrance with her sweeter breath;
The while her haughty lips more beautifully swell

" With consciousness of every charm's excess;
While with becoming scorn she turned her face
From every eye that darted its caress,
As if some god alone might hope for her embrace.

LXXII.

" Soon one, in dress of noble Median, came
Fresh from repose and from the bath; and he
To the warm fancy of so proud a dame,
Might well, as then he looked, be deemed a deity.

LXXIII.

"The tall Zameïa, seen from all apart,
  Fixed his black eye; and, as its glance she caught,
The opening lip, the involuntary start,
  Spoke more than words. The stranger saw, and sought.

LXXIV.

"And, when the priest restored her to my hands,—
  'Goddess, in thy propitiated power,
Let holy love now close her nuptial bands!'
  So prayed I as we went. But evil was the hour

"When from her home I led her: some fell star,
  That, while the sorcerer culls his herbs malign,
Favors his spell, with secret power afar
  Reigned o'er that wretched princess' birth and mine.

LXXV.

"Through all the livelong night no sleep for her:
  She called me to her couch at day's first beam,
But not on lord or palace to confer:
  Stranger and festival,—she would no other theme.

LXXVI.

"I lent her bath of perfume every art;
  I spread her banquet of the choicest store;
I bade her women touch their lutes apart,
  And told her tales she never heard before.

LXXVII.

"Warbled her birds, her bubbling fountains played;
But bath and banquet all untouched remain;
And to her maidens trilling in the shade
She called impatiently to close the strain.

LXXVIII.

" And all in her neglected charms she lay:
Fever was in her veins; her pulse beat high;
And on the morning of the second day
She said, 'Neantes, wilt thou see me die?'

LXXIX.

"'Die!' (so I spoke.) 'Venus forfend such sight!'
'Then, if thou wilt not, O my friend!' (she said,)
'Go find the lovely Median ere 'tis night:
Nay, dear Neantes, here upon this bed

"'Else will I spill my blood. The wall is low
Nearest Euphrates, where pomegranates bloom
Among the orange-trees. Nay, wilt not go?
Look upon this! and who shall tell my doom

"'To Imlec?' Then that dagger, keen and bright,
She drew from 'neath her robe, and bade me be
Content to go and find the Mede ere night.—
Lord Imlec, this was treachery to thee!

LXXX.

"But well I knew Zameïa; was afraid,
And bowed me to the earth, and said, 'Then be,
Thou dearest wife of him I serve, obeyed,
Though to destruction both of thee and me.'

LXXXI.

"She took the ruby from her neck: 'Give this;
'Tis red like my life-blood, and he will know'
(She said, and gave the jewel many a kiss)
'Upon whose bosom he beheld it glow.'

LXXXII.

"Then as a beggar, all in humble guise,
I sat me on the palace-steps, and thence
Beheld the stranger of the sparkling eyes
Late as he came from kingly audience.

LXXXIII.

"Then I approached, and touched the broidered tie
That bound his sandal on: he turned, and knew
The crimson token; took it silently,
And, quickly mingling with the crowd, withdrew.

LXXXIV.

"But when all passed, and I sat down alone,
He came again; but, for he knew his life
For slightest wrong to Imlec must atone,
Against the hope of bliss some doubt and fear made strife.

LXXXV.

"'Jewels,' he said, 'are dim to her dark eyes:
What precious gift shall match this token dear?'
'One ringlet of thy black hair she will prize,'
I said, 'beyond the gems of all Ophir.'

LXXXVI.

"Then I depicted how she wept and burned
And panted on her couch; nor, haply, more
Would rise again to life, when I returned,
If any poorer gift than love and hope I bore.

LXXXVII.

"'Great was the meed,' I said, 'the danger small;
The moon at midnight down; nor very high
Beside the river's brink her garden-wall;
And safe the path from every hand and eye.'

LXXXVIII.

"So, ere he could depart, the hour of love
Was named; and this, my little Ethiop, hung
A curious chain, of silken girdles wove,
Down from the wall where light from bended date he sprung.

LXXXIX.

"Holy Euphrates lowly murmuring swept,
As if he moaned our treachery; sadlier sang
The nightingale: her watch Zameïa kept
Until upon the flowers some being gently sprang.

XC.

"It was the Mede; and thrice returning night
With friendly veil of darkness hid their loves;
But soon again the crescent's silver light
Must shine upon the deeds of Imlec's weeping groves.

XCI.

"A light repast was set forth in a bower:
There sat Zameïa by her lover's side,
With heart of bliss so full, it had not power
Or space for even a thought of all that might betide.

XCII.

"But Meles said, 'Should I return no more,
Wouldst thou this love's excess, so dear to me,
For white-haired Imlec's coming keep in store?
Or should some other brave the peril scorned for thee?

XCIII.

"'Were it not better, if my soul could tear
It from thy sight, that Meles went his way
In peace to seek some other humbler fair?
Princess, my life and thine are forfeit if I stay.'

XCIV.

"Zameïa, paler than the ivory white
That formed the pillars of her couch, exclaimed,
'Do I not love thee more than life or light?
And have I lived to hear *another* named?

XCV.

"'Imlec to thee is nought! and all in vain
His love for me: 'tis Meles I adore.
If danger come, be mine the care and pain!
Another!—let me die, or hear that word no more!'

XCVI.

"'My own, my bright Zameïa's truth,' he said:
''Twas spoken but to prove.' And then he smiled,
And her, all trembling, to the banquet led;
And love and hope are twins, and so she was beguiled.

XCVII.

"Another midnight saw them as before,
With banquet spread, and wine the lip to woo.
Zameïa, 'neath her robe's adornment, wore
A steel half hid in gems: he saw it sparkle through.

XCVIII.

"But well he knew (with all the tenderness
Meet for a heart whose fires so fiercely burn)
To hush her doubts. With many a false caress
He went, and many an oath and promise of return.

XCIX.

"The bower is lit; the banquet waits; and wake
Love's votaress and her trembling slave: but where
The lover wont to come, and scarce partake
E'en of the grape's sweet blood for gazing on his fair?

"Lone passed the night. My beauteous mistress faints
Upon her couch, or fills the frighted ears
Of every slave with passionate complaints;
For darkly to her soul her boding fate appears.

C.

"Another midnight: still he had not come:
And thus she me reproached: 'All had been bliss,
Neantes, but for thee. Is this my doom?
And was I made an offering but for this?'

CI.

"'Alas!' I answered, 'I am but a slave,
Princess, and thine: destroy me if thou wilt.
Shall I go look for him the goddess gave?
Or for thy pleasure shall my blood be spilt?'

CII.

"The frailest hope is better than despair,
And many a life a timely word has saved.
She bade me to the palace, but not there
To find her Median more: the stream that laved

"The garden where they met, at early morn
To his own land had seen him on his way:
Nor word nor token left he, to be borne
To her who, for his sake, sickened at light of day.

CIII.

" But that it had been death to tell her *then*.
What means to save, alas! could I employ?
That moment came beneath a column's shade,
To rest a while, a dusky Arab boy.

CIV.

" Quick came the thought. I gave him gold, and craved
A cluster of his locks: he gave me one,
And black as earth-hid ebony it waved
Like those of Meles: thanks to thee, O Sun!

CV.

" In childhood once, slave to a scribe, I sought
To trace the character, and shape the reed;
And sometimes, when my lord beheld, he taught
A little of his art; and now it served my need.

CVI.

" The choicest of the Arab's locks I clipt,
And framed a letter as from Meles' hand;
Then a black ringlet, first in perfumes dipt,
Laid in the midst: nor words more sweet and bland

" Could Meles of the honey lip indite:
'Twas written on papyrus of the Nile,
Fragrant with rose; as opening lotos white;
And gold and silver dust in sprinkles o'er it smile.

CVII.

" 'Neath the pomegranates in the orange-shade,
  Where lingered last the Median (such my plan),
Among the falling blossoms it was laid
  In secret, ere I came; and thus, in promise, ran: —

CVIII.

" 'Radiant Zameïa, think upon the pain
  I bear in telling thee how many a night
Must pass ere back to Babylon again
  I come to yield my life to thy delight.

" 'My soul is sick with absence, while the will
  Of an unpitying sovereign bids me wait.
Preserve a little of love's balm to heal
  Thy Meles, who returns at gathering of the date.'

CIX.

" So, when among the flowers the scroll was flung,
  Sadly I came at having found him not;
And near that wall, where silken chain was hung,
  I drew Zameïa. On the very spot

" Where her loved Meles spoke his last farewell
  That princess kissed a camel-driver's hair!
And tears of joy (ah, too fallacious!) fell
  On what a slave's poor hand had placed in pity there.

CX.

"Yet, though 'twas sad to see her so deceived,
I could but bless the tears her cheek was drinking;
For pity framed the falsehood hope believed,
And so by this slight reed her soul was saved from sinking.

CXI.

"The gathering of the sweet and savory date
Approached, and Imlec still was far away.
Zameïa learned to wait and hope and wait,
And blessed the powerful Belus for his stay.

CXII.

"But as the date-tree sees her blossoms die,
And blasted on the earth her fruit's soft germ,
Unless her vegetable love come nigh
With genial power while yet endures her term;

CXIII.

"So poor Zameïa's hopes, like date-buds, down
Must fall to earth unblest and immature:
Alas! unless her Meles come to crown
With fruit, hope's blossoms cannot long endure!

CXIV.

"The date was ripe and plucked; but still there came
No beauteous Mede. Zameïa raged and pined,
And pined and hoped and wept. What could I frame?
With what new bland deceit bedew her withering mind?

CXV.

"Night after night she waked and waked: consumed
Her full round arms; no tulip hue upon
Her sunny cheek in changeful beauty bloomed:
She felt a dearth, a blight, and all was cold and wan.

"I trembled for her life: so when one day
She glided, pale, where full pomegranates glowed,
Among the leaves another letter lay;
And thus, as kindly as the first, it flowed:—

CXVI.

"'Adored Zameïa! if thou still dost bear
Enough of love to feel a moment's pain
That Meles, still detained by toil and care,
Comes not to thee and Babylon again,

"'Though dates be plucked, I prithee wait a span:
For, when rich spices from Arabia's hills
Load for thy happy streets the caravan,
I come to keep the word my panting soul fulfils.'

CXVII.

"I need not tell who placed the letter there;
And though her reason made some little strife,
By sending doubt 'gainst hope, yet from despair
A while her heart emerged; and so was saved her life.

CXVIII.

"Again she bathed her limbs, and ate her food,
And bound her streaming hair, and clasped her zone.
Like the wild courser by his wants subdued,
So stooped her soul to feed on this poor hope alone.

CXIX.

"The Median had but lightly loved; while she
Inhaled a flame that never ceased to prey
Upon her victim heart: she ceased to be,
And, severed from herself, became, that day,

"Appendage to another. Not the string
Of Meles' sandal, scarf about his waist,
Or feather for his arrows, was a thing
More wholly his than she, so proud ere love debased!

CXX.

"Euphrates' floods are swollen with timely rain;
Cassia and myrrh perfume the crowded streets;
The burthen from the camel's back is ta'en:
But Meles' footsteps press no flower in our retreats.

CXXI.

"Most wretched princess! who her state can show?
Panting with haste, a messenger arrives
To tell (oh full completion of her woe!)
That Imlec's on his way, and bids prepare his wives.

CXXII.

"'Hide me,' she said, 'in some dark desert cave,
Till I can look a moment on my love!
Cast me, Neantes, to Euphrates' wave
Ere Imlec come! — O Venus! can I prove

"'For Meles' ardor frenzy of the grape,
The poppy's fetid juice for Meles' breath? —
Save me, Neantes! aid me to escape!
If Imlec clasp at all, he clasps me cold in death!'

CXXIII.

"Her forceful words were true: her pale, pale cheek
And tearless eye too strong concurrence gave;
And o'erwrought passion left her form so weak,
But little more had laid it in the grave.

CXXIV.

"A curious cincture by her mother wrought,
Twined with a tress of her black hair, was thrown
To the full stream to baffle those who sought,
That by no vestige might our course be known.

CXXV.

"Enough to tell, upon a fearful night,
By the same silken chain that Meles prest,
The garden wall was scaled. Our piteous plight,
This place, O stranger! must declare the rest."

CUBA: PUEBLO NUEVO, September, 1828.

CANTO SIXTH.

BRIDAL OF HELON.

ARGUMENT.

Twilight. — Egla alone in her grove of acacias. — Zóphiël returns wounded and dejected, and sits watching her invisibly. — A being, who wishes to preserve Egla, perceives that she is beset with dangers. — Zameïa dies in attempting the life of Egla. — Egla is reproached by a slave, faints, and is supported by Helon: Helon and Hariph bear her home. — Egla, about to destroy herself, is saved by Helon, who receives her in marriage, and puts Zóphiël to flight by means of a carneol box. — Hariph discovers himself to be the angel Raphaël; seeks Zóphiël in the deserts of Ethiopia, and speaks to him of hope and comfort.

BRIDAL OF HELON.

I.

SWEET is the evening twilight; but, alas!
There's sadness in it: day's light tasks are done;
And leisure sighs to think how soon must pass
Those tints that melt o'er heaven, O setting Sun!

And look like heaven dissolved. A tender flush
Of blended rose and purple light o'er all
The luscious landscape spreads, — like pleasure's blush, —
And glows o'er wave, sky, flower, and palm-tree tall.

II.

'Tis now that solitude has most of pain:
Vague apprehensions of approaching night
Whisper the soul attuned to bliss, and fain
To find in love equivalent for light.

III.

The bard has sung, God never formed a soul
  Without its own peculiar mate, to meet
Its wandering half, when ripe to crown the whole
  Bright plan of bliss, most heavenly, most complete.

IV.

But thousand evil things there are that hate
  To look on happiness: these hurt, impede,
And, leagued with time, space, circumstance, and fate,
  Keep kindred heart from heart, to pine and pant and
    bleed.

And as the dove to far Palmyra flying
  From where her native founts of Antioch beam,
Weary, exhausted, longing, panting, sighing,
  Lights sadly at the desert's bitter stream;

So many a soul o'er life's drear desert faring, —
  Love's pure congenial spring unfound, unquaffed, —
Suffers, recoils; then, thirsty and despairing
  Of what it would, descends, and sips the nearest draught.

V.

'Tis twilight in fair Egla's grove: her eye
  Is sad and wistful; while the hues that glint
In soft profusion o'er the molten sky
  O'er all her beauty spread a mellower tint.

VI.

And, formed in every fibre for such love
  As Heaven not yet had given her to share,
Through the deep shadowy vistas of her grove
  Sent looks of wistfulness. No Spirit there

Appears as wont: for many a month so long
  He had not left her: what could so detain?
She took her lute, and tuned it for a song,
  The while spontaneous words accord them to a strain

Taught by enamoured Zóphiël: softly heaving
  The while her heart, thus from its inmost core
Such feelings gushed, to Lydian numbers weaving,
  As never had her lip expressed before: —

VII.

SONG.

Day in melting purple dying,
Blossoms all around me sighing,
Fragrance from the lilies straying,
Zephyr with my ringlets playing,
    Ye but waken my distress:
    I am sick of loneliness.

Thou to whom I love to hearken,
Come ere night around me darken:
Though thy softness but deceive me,
Say thou'rt true, and I'll believe thee.
    Veil, if ill, thy soul's intent:
    Let me think it innocent!

Save thy toiling, spare thy treasure:
All I ask is friendship's pleasure:
Let the shining ore lie darkling;
Bring no gem in lustre sparkling;
Gifts and gold are nought to me:
I would only look on thee;

Tell to thee the high-wrought feeling,
Ecstasy but in revealing;
Paint to thee the deep sensation,
Rapture in participation,
Yet but torture, if comprest
In a lone unfriended breast.

Absent still? Ah, come and bless me!
Let these eyes again caress thee.
Once, in caution, I could fly thee:
Now I nothing could deny thee.
In a look if death there be,
Come, and I will gaze on thee!

VIII.

An unknown spirit, who for many a year
Had marked in Helon passing excellence,
And loved to watch o'er Egla too, came near
This eve; but other cares had long time kept him hence.

IX.

A lute-chord sounds: hark! for a tender hymn
  To bear to heaven he pauses in his flight:
Alas! it is not heaven that lends her theme!
  Nay, if he leave her, she is lost to-night.

X.

He starts; he looks through the light, trembling shade,
  And fears, e'en now, his coming is too late:
What varied perils have beset the maid!
  She verges to the crisis of her fate.

XI.

He gazes on her guileless face, and grieves:
  There's treachery even in her own lute's sound;
And things his heavenly sense alone perceives,
  Unseen amidst the flowers lurk close around.

XII.

And Zóphiël too, late from the deep returned
  In such a state 'twas piteous but to see,
Watched near the maid — whose love he fain had earned
  By fiercer torments still — invisibly.

XIII.

His wings were folded o'er his eyes: severe
  As was the pain he'd borne from wave and wind,
The dubious warning of that Being drear
  Who met him in the lightning, to his mind

Was torture worse: a dark presentiment
Came o'er his soul with paralyzing chill,
As when Fate vaguely whispers her intent
To poison mortal joy with sense of pending ill.

XIV.

He searched about the grove with all the care
Of trembling jealousy, as if to trace
By track or wounded flower some rival there;
And scarcely dared to look upon the face

Of her he loved, lest it some tale might tell
To make the only hope that soothed him vain.
He hears her notes in numbers die and swell,
But almost fears to listen to the strain

Himself had taught her, lest some hated name
Had been with that dear gentle air inwreathed
While he was far. She sighed: he nearer came:
Oh transport! Zóphiël was the name she breathed!

XV.

He saw but her, and thought her all alone:
His name was on her lip in hour like this!
And, doting, — drinking every look and tone, —
Paused, ere he would advance, for very bliss.

XVI.

The joy of a whole mortal life he felt
In that one moment. Now, too long unseen,

He fain had shown his beauteous form, and knelt;
  But, while he still delayed, a mortal rushed between.

XVII.

Tall was her form; her quivering lip was pale;
  Long streamed her hair; and glared her wild dark eye;
And, grasping Egla's arm, — "No arts avail
  Thee now! Vile murderess of my Meles, die!"

She said: her dagger at soft Egla's breast
  Touched the white folded robe; but, failing breath
And strength, at once that frenzied arm arrest;
  And, sinking to the earth, Zameïa groaned in death.

XVIII.

This Orpha saw, — a slave, a sullen maid,
  But beautiful; whose glance Rosanes caught
While yet the captives at the palace staid,
  And secretly caressed until he taught

The haughty girl, impatient of her fate,
  A hope that gave her, in her lowliness,
The wild ambition of a higher state.
  But who can paint the depth of her distress,

When he had gone to seek the dangerous bride,
  And when the following morn his death revealed?
Hate, envy, love, sorrow, hopes crushed, — all vied
  To nurture the revenge her withering heart concealed.

XIX.

'Twas she who told Zameïa of the doom
Of her loved Mede, and led her to the breast
She burned to pierce. Now from her heart of gloom
Burst the deep smouldering rage thus bitterly expressed:—

XX.

"Another murder! Sorceress, to me
Tell not a Spirit did it: I know well
What wanton thing thou art: was't not by thee
Rosanes, Meles, young Altheëtor fell,

"Lured by thine arts to glut a love as dread
As that fell queen's, who every morning spilt
The separate life that warmed her nightly bed,
Closing, with death's cold seal, lips that might tell her guilt?"

XXI.

Then came Neantes, knelt, and bathed with tears
The lost Zameïa's form: 'twas dim and cold;
But the strong cast of beauty still appears,
Though o'er her brow the last chill dews had rolled.

XXII.

And, as he held the taper hand in his
Of his loved mistress (with a piteous look
On Egla cast), his sole reproach was this,
Half checked by rising sobs that burst forth as he spoke:—

XXIII.

"Oh! warm with health and beauty as thou art,
Couldst thou have seen her as I have, — then reft
Of all, — and known the torments of her heart,
Thou hadst not ta'en what little life was left."

XXIV.

The attempted deed, the scene, the bitter word,
Like knot of serpents, each with separate sting,
Pierced, each and all, more keenly than a sword,
Through Egla's heart, that bled while answering: —

"Cease, cease! I killed her not, nor knew such one
There lived on earth. Alas! her purpose rough,
Would to high Heaven, ere she had died, were done! —
O Power that formed me! was it not enough

"To bear perpetual solitude and gloom?
Must I, too, live a theme of foul reproach
To stranger and to slave? The tomb, the tomb,
Is all I ask! Oh! do I ask too much?"

XXV.

She said, and swooned: so Helon, not in vain,
Searched wandering for his guide (he knew not whither),
To lead him to the gates of Ecbatane;
And haply, though unseen, his guide had led him hither.

XXVI.

He saw Zameïa on the earth laid low;
And Egla, faint, but fresh in all her charms,
Had sunk beside the corse for weight of woe
But for the timely aid of his receiving arms.

XXVII.

The group, the dead, the form his arms sustain,
The trembling leaves, the twilight's fading gleam,
Confuse: the youth distrusts both eye and brain;
For 'gainst his heart he sees the image of his dream.

XXVIII.

But faithful Hariph soon was at his side,
In search of whom had Helon chanced to roam:
"Ask nothing, youth, but haste with me!" he cried.
"Life has not left the maiden: bear her home."

XXIX.

They laid her her on her couch, and in her sire
Found him they sought, and in her dwelling staid.
Sèphora sat her by the perfumed fire
All night, and watched her child, yet sore afraid

Of her enamoured Spirit, — well she knew
The presence of a mortal vexed his will, —
And mused on Helon's youth; and could but view,
In thought, another scene of death and ill.

XXX.

Egla lay drowned in grief, and could not speak,
  But calmed at morn the tumult of her breast,
And kissed her mother thrice; then bade her seek,
  And warn, and save from death, the stranger guest.

XXXI.

And through her window when the deepening glows
  Of pensive twilight told another day
Was spent, to bathe that fatal form she rose,
  Bound cincture o'er her robe, and sent her maids away.

XXXII.

Alone, she thought how Helon had sustained
  And saved, for his own doom, her fatal breath;
Zameïa, Orpha too: why still remained
  Her own scorned life the cause of so much death?

XXXIII.

She could not pray; and to her aching eye
  Would come no sweet relief, no wonted tear;
For one of those dark things that lurked was by,
  And whispered thoughts of horror in her ear.

XXXIV.

Then on his sad unguarded victim fixed,
  And coldly, to her wounded bosom's core,
Infused him like some fell disease, and mixed
  His being with her blood: all hope was o'er,

All fear, all nature, — all was bitterness:
She felt her heart within her like a clod;
And, when at length the sullen deep distress
Found utterance, thus she spoke ungrateful to her God: —

XXXV.

"Was but my infant life for tortures worse
Than flame or sword preserved? On me — on me —
Falls the whole burthen of my nation's curse?
Of all offence I bear the misery!

XXXVI.

"O Power that made! thou'st been profuse of pain,
And I have borne; but now is past the hour:
I ask no mitigation, — that were vain:
Wreak, wreak on me thy whole avenging power!

XXXVII.

"Yet wherefore more the doom I wish delay?
Dissolve me: oh! as earth I was before,
Change this fair-colored form to silent gray,
And let my weary organs feel no more!"

XXXVIII.

She paused: "'Tis written thus: 'Thou shalt not kill.'
Yet deeper were the crime to keep a life
Torture to me, to others death and ill:
So in thy presence, God, I end my nature's strife!"

XXXIX.

Then from her waist she took the girdle blue;
  Looked on the world without, but breathed no sigh;
Then calmly o'er the window's carving threw
  That scarf, and round her neck wound thrice the silken
    tie.

XL.

Where, in that hour, was Zóphiël? All in vain
  He burns, with love and jealous rage impelled:
With the dark Being of the storm again
  He strives and struggles in the grove, withheld

From her he loves; had seen her borne away
  Before his very eyes; and now, perforce,
Could only look where, newly murdered, lay
  The lost Zameïa's pale and breathless corse.

XLI.

Whichever Spirit conquers in the strife,
  Alas for Egla! Now her hands intwine
The guilty knot; she springs. "Hold, hold! thy life,
  Maiden, is not thine own, but God's and mine!"

XLII.

'Twas Helon's voice: but still the legate fiend,
  Reluctant to resign her, would not part;
But by his secret, subtle nature screened,
  Even from Spirits, through her brain and heart

Darted like pain. The youth with firm embrace
Holds and protects; but, writhing, vexed, and thrown,
She could not even look upon his face,
And answered all he said but with a moan.

XLIII.

Helon bent o'er, and murmured, "Calm those fears:
To be my bride already art thou given!
And I am he, who, in thy childish years,
Was in thy grove announced to thee by Heaven."

XLIV.

She seemed to listen: soon her moans were hushed;
She caught his words thus suffering and possest;
From her torn heart a grateful torrent gushed,
And love expelled the demon from her breast.

XLV.

Still Helon held, and soothed, and timely drew
Near to the vase of perfumes nightly burning,
And, from his open box of carneol, threw
All it contained. 'Twas well: Zóphiël returning,

That moment 'scaped from him whose malice held,
Rushed fiercely anxious to a scene of love
Approved by Heaven. Oh torture! he beheld
A stranger's arm intwine! Eager to prove

That power to mortal rival late so fell,
Enough had been a moment for his ire:

But a strange force he vainly strove to quell,
  Insufferable, from the perfume fire,

Rushed forth, resistless as his Maker's breath;
  And when he fain would place him by the bed,
Which, but to touch, had been gay Meles' death,
  He felt him hurled away, uttered a shriek, and fled.

XLVI.

But Helon lives, supporting still the maid
  O'erwhelmed with hopes and fears, and all o'erspent
With recent pain. "Didst hear that shriek?" he said:
  "The Sprite has left us: kneel with me!" They knelt

Them both to earth, — the bridegroom and his bride,
  So filled with present joy, the past was dim:
'Twas rapture now, whatever might betide;
  And pain to her were bliss, so it were shared with him.

XLVII.

Then prayed he: "Heaven, if either have offended,
  Punish us now! avenge! but with one breath
Let our so-late-united lives be ended!
  Let her be mine, and give me life or death!"

XLVIII.

Then she: "If now I die, I die his wife,
  And fully blest, O Heaven, await my doom!
Nor would exchange for thousand years of life
  The dearer privilege to share his tomb.

XLIX.

" Yet, if we die not, Maker, to him give
Light from thy source: so shall my sin be less
In thine account; for, oh! I ne'er can live
Other, with him, than his idolatress."

L.

" Let me adore thy image as I gaze
On her fair eyes now raised with mine to thee;
And let her find, while flow our years and days,
To feed her love, some spark of thee in me,"

LI.

(He said:) " thus, as we kneel, no wild desire
Blends with our voices in unhallowed sighs.
Spirit, to thee we quench the nuptial fire:
Look down propitious on the sacrifice!

LII.

" Receive it as a token that our love
Is of the soul; and, if our lives endure,
Spirit; who sit'st diffusing life above,
Look on our union, and pronounce it pure!"

LIII.

While thus they prayed, Hariph her kindred brought
To listen to them: thus, as, one by one,
Rose their heart-offerings, sense subdued by thought,
" This borne to heaven," he said, " my task is done.

LIV.

"Call me no longer Hariph: I but took,
For love of that young pair, this mortal guise;
And often have I stood beside Heaven's book,
And given in record there their deeds and sighs.

LV.

"From infancy I've watched them, far apart,
Oppressed by men and fiends, yet formed to dwell
Soul blent with soul, and beating heart 'gainst heart:
'Tis done. Behold the angel Raphaël!

LVI.

"That blest commission, friend of men, I bear,
To comfort those who undeservedly mourn;
And every good resolve, kind tear, heart-prayer,
'Tis mine to show before the Eternal's throne.

LVII.

"And oft I haste, and, when the good and true
Are headlong urged to deep pollution, save,
Just as my wings receive some drops of dew,
Which else must join Asphaltites' black wave,"

LVIII.

He said, all o'er to radiant beauty warming:
While they, in doubt of what they looked upon,
Beheld a form dissolving, dazzling, charming;
But, ere their lips found utterance, it was gone.

LIX.

Afar that pitying angel bent his flight,
In anxious search, revolving in his breast
Of a once heavenly brother's wretched plight:
Torn from his last dear hope, where could he rest?

LX.

Hurled 'gainst his will, the suffering Zóphiël went
To the remotest of Egyptia's bounds:
Demons pursued to view his punishment,
And with his shrieks the desert blast resounds.

LXI.

Dark shadowy fiends, invidious that he joyed
In love and beauty still, less deeply curst
Than they, of late had leagued them, and employed
All arts to crush and foil. Now, as when first

Expelled from heaven they saw him writhe, and while
He groans, and clasps the earth, sit them beside,
Ask questions of his bliss, and then with smile
Recount his baffled schemes, and linger to deride.

LXII.

And, when they fled, he hid him in a cave,
Strewn with the bones of some sad wretch, who there,
Apart from men, had sought a desert grave,
And yielded to the demon of despair.

LXIII.

There beauteous Zóphiël, shrinking from the ray,
  Envying the wretch that so his life had ended,
Wailed his eternity. He fain would pray,
  But could not pray to one he had offended.

LXIV.

The fiercest pains of death had been relief,
  And yet his quenchless being might not end.
Hark! Raphaël's voice breaks sweetly on his grief: —
  "Hope, Zóphiël! hope, hope, hope! thou hast a
    friend!"

CUBA, CAFÉTAL SAN ANDRES, January, 1829.

MISCELLANEOUS PIECES.

ODE TO THE DEPARTED.

"*Con Vistas del Cielo.*"

THE dearth is sore: the orange leaf is curled.
There's dust upon the marble o'er thy tomb,
My Edgar,[1] fair and dear:
Though the fifth sorrowing year
Hath passed since first I knew thine early doom,
I see thee still, though Death thy being hence hath hurled.

I could not bear my lot, now thou art gone,—
With heart o'er-softened by the many tears
Remorse and grief have drawn,—
Save that a gleam, a dawn
(Haply of that which lights thee now), appears
To unveil a few fair scenes of Life's next coming morn.

"What, where, is heaven?" earth's sweetest lips exclaim.
In all the holiest seers have writ or said,
Blurred are the pictures given:
We know not what is heaven,
Save by those views mysteriously spread
When the soul looks afar by light of her own flame.

[1] The son of Mrs. Brooks.

Yet all our spirits, while on earth so faint,
By glimpses dim, discern, conceive, or know,
The Eternal Power can mould
Real as fruits or gold,
Bid the celestial roseate matter glow,
And forms more perfect smile than artists carve or paint.

To realize every creed conceived
In mortal brain by love and beauty charmed—
Even like the ivory maid,
Who, as Pygmalion prayed,
Oped her white arms, to life and feeling warmed—
Would lightly task the power of life's great Chief believed.

If Grecian Phidias, in stone like this
Thy tomb, could do so much, what cannot He,
Who from the cold, coarse clod
By reckless laborer trod
Can call such tints as meeting seraphs see,
And give them breath and warmth like true love's soul-felt kiss?

Wild fears of dark annihilation, go!
Be warm, ye veins, now blackening with despair!
Years o'er thee have revolved,
My first-born; thou'rt dissolved,—
All—every tint—save a few ringlets fair:
Still, if thou didst not live, how could I love thee so?

Quick as the warmth which darts from breast to breast
  When lovers from afar each other see,
    Haply thy spirit went,
    Where mine would fain be rent,
  To take a heavenly form, designed to be
Meet dwelling for the soul thine azure eye expressed.

Thy deep blue eye! — say, can heaven's bliss exceed
  The joy of some brief moments tasted here?
    Ah! could I taste again!
    Is there a mode of pain
  Which for such guerdon could be deemed severe?
Be ours the forms of heaven, and let me bend and bleed!

To be in place, even like some spots on earth,
  In those sweet moments when no ill comes near;
    Where perfumes round us wreathe,
    And the pure air we breathe
  Nerves and exhilarates; while all we hear
So tells content and love, we sigh, and bless our birth;

To clasp thee, Edgar, in a fragrant shape
  Of fair perfection, after death's sad hour,
    Known as the same I've prest
    Erst to this aching breast, —
  The same, but finished by a kind, bland Power,
Which only stopped thy heart to let thy soul escape, —

Oh ! every pain that vexed thy mortal life,
  Nay, even the lives of all who round me lie, —
    Be this one bliss my share,
    The whole condensed I'll bear,
  Bless the benign creative hand, and sigh,
And kneel to ask again the expiatory strife, —

Strife, for the hope of making others blest,
  Who trespassed only that they were not brave
    Enough to bear or take
    Pains, even for pity's sake, —
  Strife, for the hope to wake, incite, and save
Even those who, dull with crime, know not fair Honor's zest.

If in the pauses of my agony
  (Be it or flame, stab, scourge, or pestilence),
    If, fresh and blest as dear,
    Thou'lt come in beauty near,
  Speak, and with looks of love charm my keen sense,
I'll deem it heaven enough even thus to feel and see ;

To feel my hand wrenched as with mortal rack,
  Then see it healed, and ta'en, and kindly prest,
    And fair as blossoms white
    Of cerea in the night ;
  While tears that fall upon thy spotless breast
Are sweet as drops from flowers touched in thy heavenly track !

In form to bear nor stain nor scar designed, —
  Yes! let me kneel to agonize again;
    Ask every torment o'er
    More poignant than before:
  Of a whole world the price of a whole pain
Were small for such blest gifts of matter and of mind!

Comes a cold doubt, — that still thou art alive,
  Edgar, my heart tells, while these numbers thrill,
    Yet of a bliss so dear,
    And as Death's portal's near
  I feel me too unworthy: dreary Time,
I fear, must bear his part ere Hope her plight fulfil!

Time, time was meet (so many a sacred scroll
  Has told and tells) ere light was bid to smile;
    Ere yet the spheres, revealed,
    Gave music as they wheeled;
  Warm, rife, eternal love — a time — a while —
Brooded and charmed and ranged till chaos gloomed no more.

As time was needful ere a world could bloom
  With forms of flowers and flesh, haply must wait
    Some spirits; and, lingering still,
    Of deeds both good and ill
  Mark the effect in intermediate state,
And think and pause and weep even over their own tomb.

Be it so: if, thin as fragrance, light, or heat,
Thine essence, floating on the ambient air,
Can with freed intellect
View every deed's effect,
Read even my heart in all its pantings bare,
When denser pulses cease, how sweet even thus to meet;

To roam those deep green aisles crowned with tall palms,
And weep for all who tire of toil and ill,
While moons of winter bring
Their blossoms fair as spring;
To move, unseen by all we've left, and will
Such influence to their souls as half their pain becalms;

On deep Mohecan's[1] mounts to view the spot
Where, as these arms were oped to clasp thee, came
The tidings, dread and cold,
I nevermore might hold
Thy pulsing form, nor meet the gentle flame
Of thy fair eyes till mine for those of earth were not;

On precipice where the gray citadel
Hangs over Ladaüanna's[2] billows clear,
How sweet to pause and view
As erst the far canoe;
To glide by friends who know not we are near,
And hear them of ourselves in tender memory tell;

[1] "Mohecan," aboriginal name of the Hudson.
[2] "Ladaüanna," aboriginal name of the St. Lawrence.

Or, where Niagara with maddening roar
  Shakes the worn cliff, haply to flit, and ken
    Some angel, as he sighs
    With pleasure at the dyes
  Of the wild depth, while to the eyes of men
Invisible we speak by signs unknown before;

Or, far from this wild Western world, where dwelt
  That brow whose laurels bore a leaf for mine,
    When, strong in sympathy,
    Thy sprite shall roam with me,
  Edgar, 'mid Derwent's flowers, one soul benign
May to thy soul impart the joy I there have felt!

What though, "imprisoned in the viewless winds,"
  'Mid storms and rocks, like earthly ship, we're dashed,
    Unsevered while we're blent,
    We'll bear in sweet content
  The shock of falling bolt or forest crashed,
While thoughts of hope and love nerve well our mystic minds.

Wafted or wandering thus, souls may be found
  Or ripe for forms of heaven, or for that state
    Of which, when angels think,
    Or saints, they weep and shrink,
  And oft, to draw or save from such dread fate,
Are fain their beauteous heads to dash 'gainst blood-stained ground.

Freed from their earthly gyves, if spirits laugh
  And shriek with horrid joy when victims bleed
    Or suffer as we view
    Mortals in vileness do,
  The Eternal and his court may keep their meed
Of joy: far other cups fell thirsty Guilt must quaff!

O Edgar! spirit or on earth or air,
  Seen or impalpable to artist's sketch,
    In essence or in form,
    In bliss, pain, calm, or storm,
  Let us, wherever met a suffering wretch,
Task every power to shield and save him from despair!

Nature hath secrets mortals ne'er suspect:
  At some we glance, while some are sealed in night.
    The optician, by his skill,
    Even now can show at will
  Long-absent pheers in shapes of moving light:
If man so much can do, what cannot Heaven effect!

Shade, image, manes, all the ancient priest
  Told to his votarists in fraud or zeal,
    May be, and might have been
    By means and arts we ween
  No more of, in this age: for woe or weal
Of man, full much foreknown, to this late race hath ceased.

That souls may take ambrosial forms in heaven,
A dawning science half assures the hope:
These forms may sleep and smile
Midst heaven's fresh roses, while
Their spirits free roam o'er this world's whole scope
For pleasure and for good, Heaven's full permission given.

I have not sung of meeting those we've loved
Or known, and listening to their accents meek,
While pitying all they've pained
On earth, while passion reigned,
To wreak redress upon themselves they seek,
And bless, for each stern deed, the pain they now have proved.

I have not sung of the first, fairest court
Of all those mansions; of the heavenly home,
Of which the best hath told
Who e'er trod earthly mould:
To courts of earthly kings the fairest come
Haply to show faint types of this supreme resort.

Haply the Sire of sires may take a form,
And give an audience to each set unfurled
With bands of sympathy,
Wreathen in mystery,
Round those who've known each other in this world,
Perfecting all the rest, and breathing beauty warm.

Essence, light, heat, form, throbbing arteries,—
  To deem each possible, enough I see!
    Edgar, thou knowest I wait:
    Guard my expectant state;
  Console me, as I bend in prayers for thee;
Aid me, even as thou mayest, both Heaven and thee to please!

This song to thee alone! Though he who shares
  Thy bed of stone shared well my love with thee,
    Yet in his noble heart
    Another bore a part,
  Whilst thou hadst never other love than me:
Sprites, brothers, manes, shades, present my tears and prayers!

NOTE.—Mr. Griswold says, in his "Female Poets of America" (1853), that the above peculiar stanza was invented by Maria del Occidente.

FAREWELL TO CUBA.

ADIEU, fair isle! I love thy bowers:
  I love thy dark-eyed daughters there;
The cool pomegranate's scarlet flowers
  Look brighter in their jetty hair.

They praised my forehead's stainless white,
  And, when I thirsted, gave a draught
From the full clustering cocoa's height,
  And, smiling, blessed me as I quaffed.

Well pleased, the kind return I gave,
  And, clasped in their embraces' twine,
Felt the soft breeze, like Lethe's wave,
  Becalm this beating heart of mine.

Why will my heart so wildly beat?
  Say, seraphs, is my lot too blest,
That thus a fitful, feverish heat
  Must rifle me of health and rest?

Alas! I fear my native snows:
  A clime too cold, a heart too warm, —
Alternate chills, alternate glows, —
  Too fiercely threat my flower-like form.

The orange-tree has fruit and flowers;
The grenadilla in its bloom
Hangs o'er its high, luxuriant bowers,
Like fringes from a Tyrian loom.

When the white coffee-blossoms swell,
The fair moon full, the evening long,
I love to hear the warbling bell,
And sunburnt peasant's wayward song.

Drive gently on, dark muleteer,
And the light seguidilla frame:
Fain would I listen still to hear
At every close thy mistress' name.

Adieu, fair isle! the waving palm
Is pencilled on thy purest sky:
Warm sleeps the bay, the air is balm,
And, soothed to languor, scarce a sigh

Escapes for those I love so well,
For those I've loved and left so long:
On me their fondest musings dwell,
To them alone my sighs belong.

On, on, my bark! blow, southern breeze!
No longer would I lingering stay:
'Twere better far *to die* with these
Than *live in pleasure* far away.

CUBA, April, 1827.

NOTES TO ZÓPHIËL.

NOTES TO CANTO FIRST.

GROVE OF ACACIAS.

Page 3, Verse 1, Line 3.

" The selfsame breeze that passes o'er thy breast."

The remains of Columbus are preserved in the cathedral at Havana, beneath a monument and bust of very rude sculpture. These stanzas were written on the same coast, about seventy miles distant.

Page 3, Verse 2, Line 1.

" Madoc, my ancient fathers' bones repose
Where their bold harps thy country's bards inwreathed."

The well-known and beautiful poem of Dr. Robert Southey, which bears the name of the Welch prince Madoc, renders it unnecessary to give any further account of him.

Page 5, Verse 4, Line 3.

From the cessation of oracles at the death of the Founder of our religion, the old Christian fathers inferred that the demons who uttered them were at that time confined.

PAGE 8, VERSE 5, LINE 2.

Twenty years, among the Spartans, was the age required by the law for the marriage of women; and, in whatever climate they may live, it is seldom that they attain their full height and proportion before that age. If this custom of the Spartans could be everywhere observed, it is probable the strength and beauty of the race would be improved by it.

PAGE 9, VERSE 3, LINE 1.

Some of the acacias of the East are endowed with a sensitive power, and are said to bend gently over those who seek their shade.

PAGE 9, VERSE 4, LINE 3.

"And here the full cerulean passion-flower,
Climbing among the leaves, its mystic symbols hung."

Those who have only seen this flower as a curious exotic in severer climates can have little idea of the profusion with which it grows in its native realms. It climbs from shrub to shrub, forming natural bowers, sparkling with morning dew, and looking, from its beamy shape, like a beautiful planet.

PAGE 10, VERSE 3, LAST LINE.

It is impossible for those who never felt it to conceive the effect of such a situation in a warm climate. In this island, the woods, which are naturally so interwoven with vines as to be impervious to a human being, are in some places cleared and converted into nurseries for the young coffee-trees, which remain sheltered from the sun and wind till sufficiently grown to transplant. To enter one of these "semilleros," as they are here called, at noonday, produces an effect like that anciently ascribed to the waters of Lethe. After sitting down upon the trunk of a fallen cedar or palm-tree, and breathing for a moment the freshness of the air and the odor of the passion-flower, — which is one of the most abundant and certainly the most beautiful of the climate, — the noise of the trees, which are continually kept in motion by the trade-winds; the fluttering and various notes (though not musical) of the birds; the loftiness of the green canopy (for the trunks of the trees are bare to a great height, and seem like pillars supporting a thick mass of leaves above); and the soft, peculiar light which the intense ray of the sun, thus impeded, produces, — have altogether such an effect, that one seems involuntarily to forget every thing but the present, and it requires a strong effort to rise and leave the place.

Page 12, Last Verse, Line 3.

"The palm is a very common plant in this country (Media), and generally fruitful: this they cultivate like fig-trees; and it produces them bread, wine, and honey." — See Beloe's notes to his translation of Herodotus. Mr. Gibbon adds that the diligent natives celebrated either in verse or prose three hundred and sixty uses to which the trunk, the branches, the leaves, the juice, and the whole of this plant, were applied. Nothing can be more curious and interesting than the natural history of the palm-tree.

Page 13, Last Verse, Line 1.

The women among all the nations of antiquity were accustomed to express violent grief by tearing their hair. This must have been a great and affecting sacrifice to the object bemoaned, as they considered it a part of themselves, and absolutely essential to their beauty. Fine hair has been a subject of commendation among all people, and particularly the ancients. Cyrus, when he went to visit his uncle Astyages, found him with his eyelashes colored, and decorated with false locks. The first Cæsar obtained permission to wear the laurel wreath in order to conceal the bareness of his temples. The quantity and beauty of the hair of Absalom are commemorated in Holy Writ. The modern Oriental ladies also set the greatest value on their hair, which they braid and perfume. Thus the poet Hafiz, whom Sir William Jones styles the Anacreon of Persia:—

"These locks, each curl of which is worth a hundred musk-bags of China, would be sweet indeed if their scent proceeded from sweetness of temper."

And again: "When the breeze shall waft the fragrance of thy locks over the tomb of Hafiz, a thousand flowers shall spring from out the earth that hides his corse."

Achilles clipped his yellow locks, and then threw them as a sacrifice upon the funeral pyre of Patroclus. The women of the aborigines of America cut off locks of their long black hair, and strew them upon the graves of their husbands.

Page 20, First Two Lines.

"*That, close inclining o'er her, seemed to reck*
What 'twas they canopied."

This kind of acacia, or mimosa, particularly belongs to Abyssinia: it is said to incline its branches, as if sensible, when any one seeks its shade. The Arabians love it as a friend. A low species of mimosa, which grows profusely in this island (Cuba), is extremely sensitive: it not only shuts its pretty leaves like a closed fan when touched, but the whole branch which supports them stoops, and clings closely to the main stalk.

The affection of "Aswad" for a mimosa that bent over him in the gardens of Shedad or Irem forms a particularly beautiful passage in "Thalaba."

Page 20, Verse 4, Last Line.

Every one must have observed this effect in little children, who for several hours after they have cried themselves to sleep, and sometimes even when a smile is on their lips, are heard from time to time to sob.

PAGE 21, LINE 7.

"*While friendly shades the sacred rites enshroud.*"

The captive Hebrews, though they sometimes outwardly conformed to the religion of their oppressors, were accustomed to practise their own in secret.

PAGE 21, VERSE 4.

"*His heaven-invented harp he still retained.*"

The invention of the harp was ascribed by the Hebraic historians to Jubal, who, as he lived before the deluge, enjoyed, in common with others of his race, the privilege of conversing with angels, from whom he may be supposed to have received his art. That Mercury to whom the Grecians ascribed the invention of the lyre, according to the belief of the Christian fathers, might have been the son of a guilty angel.

PAGE 23, VERSE 5.

"*Weary he fainted through the toilsome hours;*
And then his mystic nature he sustained
On steam of sacrifices, breath of flowers."

"Eusèbe, dans sa 'Préparation Evangélique,' rapporte quantité de passages de Porphyre, où ce philosophe payen assure que les mauvais démons sont les auteurs des enchantemens, des philtres, et des maléfices; que le mensonge est essentiel à leur nature; qu'ils ne font que tromper nos yeux par des spectres et par des fantômes; qu'ils excitent en nous la plupart de nos passions; qu'ils ont l'ambition de vouloir passer pour des dieux; que leurs corps aëriens se nourissent de fumigations de sang répandu et de la graisse des sacrifices; qu'il n'y a qu'eux qui se mêlent de rendre des oracles, et à qui cette fonction pleine de tromperie soit tombée en partage." — FONTENELLE, *Histoire des Oracles.*

It is related also, in the "Caherman Nameh," that the Peris fed upon precious odors brought them by their companions when imprisoned and hung up in cages by the Dives.

Most of the Oriental superstitions harmonize perfectly with the belief of the fathers; and what is there in philosophy, natural or moral, to disprove the existence of beings similar to those described by the latter?

Page 23, Verse 6.

"Sometimes he gave out oracles."

This passage accords with a belief prevalent in the earlier ages of Christianity, that all nations, except the descendants of Abraham, were abandoned by the Almighty, and subjected to the power of demons or evil spirits. Fontenelle, in his "Histoire des Oracles," makes the following extract from the works of the Pagan philosopher Porphyry: "Auguste déjà vieux et songeant à se choisir un successeur alla consulter l'Oracle de Delphes. L'Oracle ne répondait point, quoiqu' Auguste n'épargnât pas des sacrifices. A la fin, cependant, il en tira cette réponse. L'enfant Hebreu à qui tous les Dieux obéissent, me chasse d'ici, et me renvoie dans les Enfers. Sors de ce temple sans parler!"

Page 23, Last Verse.

The identity of Zóphiël with Apollo will be perceived in this and other passages.

Page 25, Verse 1.

"Still true
To one dear theme, my full soul, flowing o'er,
Would find no room for thought of what it knew,
Nor, picturing forfeit transport, curse me more."

"Si l'homme" (says a modern writer), "constant dans ses affection, pouvait sans cesse fournir à un sentiment renouvelé sans cesse, sans doute la solitude et l'amour l'égaleraient à Dieu même; car ce sont là les deux éternels plaisirs du grand Etre."

St. Theresa used to describe the Prince of Darkness as an unhappy being who never could know what it was to love.

PAGE 26, VERSE 4, LINE 1.

Zóphiël, being one of the angels who fell before the creation was completed, is not supposed to know any thing of the immortality of the souls of men.

PAGE 28, VERSE 2, LINE 3.

Cœlestes, or the Moon, was adored by many of the Jewish women, as well as the Carthaginians. They addressed their vows to her, burnt incense, poured out drink-offerings, and made cakes for her with her own hands. This goddess is called, in Scripture, the Queen of Heaven.

PAGE 31, VERSE 4, LINE 4.

"Les Perses semblent être les premiers hommes connus de nous qui parlèrent des anges comme d'huissiers célestes et de porteurs d'ordres." — VOLTAIRE, *sur les Mœurs et l'Esprit des Nations.*

PAGE 33, VERSE 3, LAST LINE.

It was not unusual among the nations of the East to imitate flowers with precious stones. The Persian kings, about the time of Artaxerxes, sat, when they gave audience, under a vine, the leaves of which were formed of gold, and the grapes of emeralds. Gold is supposed by some of the Asiatics to have grown like a tree in the Garden of Eden, and the veins of ore found in the earth still correspond to the form of branches. Shedad, in the gardens of his wonderful palace, had trees formed of gold and silver, with fruit and blossoms of precious stones. This palace, the Arabs suppose, still exists in the desert, where, though generally invisible, individuals from time to time have been indulged with a sight of it.

PAGE 33, VERSE 4, LINE 3.

"Sister" was an affectionate appellation used by the Hebrews to women.

PAGE 34, VERSE 4.

"*And o'er her sense, as when the fond night-bird*
Wooes the full rose, o'erpowering fragrance stole."

This allusion is familiar to every one in the slightest degree acquainted with Oriental literature.

"The nightingale, if he sees the rose, becomes intoxicated: he lets go from his hands the reins of prudence."—*Fable of the Gardener and Nightingale.*

Lady Montagu also translates a song thus:—

"The nightingale now hovers amid the flowers.
His passion is to seek roses."

Again, from the poet Hafiz:—

"When the roses wither, and the bower loses its sweetness,
You have no longer the tale of the nightingale."

Indeed, the rose, in Oriental poetry, is seldom mentioned without her paramour, the nightingale; which gives reason to suppose that the nightingale, in those countries where it was first celebrated, had really some natural fondness for that flower, or perhaps for some insect which took shelter in it. In Sir W. Jones's translation of the Persian fable of "The Gardener and Nightingale" is the following distich:—

"I know not what the rose says under his lips, that he brings back the helpless nightingales, with their mournful notes.

"One day the gardener, according to his established custom, went to view the roses: he saw a plaintive nightingale rubbing his head on the leaves of the roses, and tearing asunder with his sharp bill that volume adorned with gold."

And Geláleddîn Rúzbehár:—

"While the nightingale sings thy praises with a loud voice, I am all ear, like the stalk of the rose-tree."

Pliny, however, in his delightful description of this bird, says nothing, I believe, about the rose.

CUBA, CAFÉTAL SAN PATRICIO, April, 1823.

NOTES TO CANTO SECOND.

DEATH OF ALTHEËTOR.[1]

PAGE 40, LINE 2.

Chess was known at an early period. Queen Parysatis played with Artaxerxes, her son, for the life of a person whom she wished to destroy. Sir William Jones's article on the ancient game of Chaturanga, or Indian chess, is well known.

PAGE 41, VERSE 4, LINE 4.

Couches of gold and silver were not uncommon among the Median and Persian princes.

PAGE 41, VERSE 4, LINE 4.

The white and yellow jessamine is now found growing in abundance about Mount Casius, intermixed with laurels, myrtles, and other delightful shrubs.

1 This name is formed of the two Greek words *Alethes* and *etor*.

Page 41, Last Verse, Last Line.

"In every full, deep flower that crowned his paradise."

The Medes and Persians were accustomed to retire to delicious gardens, which were called paradises.

Josephus, speaking of a powerful Babylonian king, says, "He erected elevated places, for walking, of stone, and made them resemble mountains; and built them so that they might be planted with all sorts of trees. He also erected what was called a *pensile paradise*, because his wife was desirous to have things like her own country, she having been bred up in the palaces of Media."

The same custom is still continued in the East, where people of distinction pass their most pleasant hours in the pavilions or kiosks of their gardens.

Page 44, Line 5.

Sardius is the name of a precious stone.

Page 44, Verse 5, Last Line.

"And to his manes let my life-blood flow!"

Egla might have heard of the gods' manes from some wandering Ionian. The Greeks attributed four distinct parts to man,—the body, which is resolved to dust; the soul, which, as they imagined, passed to Tartarus or the Elysian Fields, according to its merits; the image, which inhabited the infernal vestibule; and the shade, which wandered about the sepulchre. This last they were accustomed to invoke three times; and libations were poured out to this as well as to the gods' manes, who were the genii of the dead, and had the care of their sepulchres and wandering shades.—*See Travels of Antenor.*

The Jews, besides, at the time this scene is supposed to have transpired, began to be imbued with the Chaldaic superstitions or belief. "The *modern* Jews," says Father Augustin Calmet, "hold the souls of men to be spiritual and immortal, but that they sometimes appear again, as well as good and evil demons; that the souls of the Hebrews are never visible either in hell or paradise, except their bodies are buried; that, even after they are buried, the soul makes frequent excursions from its destined residence to visit its former body, and inquire into its condition; that it wanders about for a full year after its first separation from the body; and that it was before the expiration of this year that the witch of Endor called up the soul of Samuel."

Origen and Theophylact say also that the Jews and Heathens believed the soul to continue near the body for some time after the death of the person. — *Calmet.*

Origen, in his second book against Celsus (continues the Reverend Father Dom Augustin Calmet), relates and subscribes to the opinion of Plato, who says "that the shadows and images of the dead, which are seen near sepulchres, are nothing but the soul disengaged from its gross body, but not yet entirely freed from matter." From the same old book, which is probably read by few, I cannot forbear transcribing the following curious account, which, however impossible, appears to have been at one time generally believed: —

"If there is any truth in what we are told by the learned Digby, chancellor to Henrietta, Queen of England, by Father Kircher, a celebrated Jesuit, by Father Schott of the same order, and by Gafferell and Vallemont, concerning the wonderful mystery of the Palingenesis, or resurrection of plants, it will help to account for the shades and phantoms which many will confidently assert they have seen in churchyards."

The account which these curious naturalists give of their performing the wonderful operation of the Palingenesis is as follows: —

"They take a flower, and burn it to ashes, from which, being collected with great care, they extract all the salts by calcination. These salts they put into a glass phial; and, having added to them a certain composition which has a property of putting the ashes in motion upon the application of heat, the whole becomes a fine dust of a bluish color. From this dust, when agitated by a gentle heat, there arise gradually a stalk, leaves, and then a flower; in short, there is seen the apparition of a plant rising out of the ashes. When the heat ceases the whole show disappears, and the dust falls into its former chaos at the bottom of the vessel. The return of heat always raises out of its ashes this vegetable phœnix, which derives its life from the presence of this genial warmth, and dies as soon as it is withdrawn."

Then follows the manner in which Father Kircher endeavors to account for the wonderful phenomenon; and the author continues with an assertion that the members of the Royal Society at London had (as he was informed) made the same experiment upon a sparrow, and were then hoping to make it succeed upon men.

Page 46, Verse 5.

The Medes, as well as the Persians, were expert with the bow and javelin.

Page 49, Verse 4.

" Yet 'such things are.'"

In the whole catalogue of all the crimes and cruelties ever recorded since the invention of letters, there is nothing so horrid to the imagination as the simple fact of the existence of desire in the immediate presence of death and carnage. Peter the Great, Czar of Muscovy, killed several of his soldiers with his own hand, at the taking of Narva, to prevent the same atrocity related of Philomars in the text.

"Jornandés reconte" (says M. de Châteaubriand), "que des sorcières chassées loin des habitations des hommes dans les déserts de la Scythie, furent visitées par des démons, et de ce commerce sortirent la nation des Huns." Deeds are still done which might well serve to prove a similar origin.

Page 50, Verse 3, Last Line.

When the Persians celebrate their feast of roses.

PAGE 50, VERSE 4.

"And snow-white Egla, mild and chaste and fair,
Came o'er his fancy."

The love of Sardius for Egla resembles that of Cyrus for Aspasia or Milto, of whom the Chevalier de Lentier gives the following account: "Aspasia, being brought to Sardis by one of the satraps of Cyrus, was compelled to come into the presence of that prince with many other women. While the rest by every art endeavored to attract his attention, Milto stood at a distance, with her eyes fixed upon the earth; and Cyrus was so charmed with the singularity of her modesty (or, more probably, of her beauty), that he dismissed all beside, and remained a long time attached to this favorite."

PAGE 52, VERSE 1, LAST LINE.

Many of the young men of Asia, and even those of Athens, used the same arts at their toilets as the women.

PAGE 52, VERSE 3.

" With black
To tip the eyelid; stain the finger; deck
The cheek with hues that languor bids it lack."

The arts practised by women to heighten their beauty were supposed to have been taught them by fallen angels.

" Dans le livre de la parure des femmes, chap. 2, Tertullien explique, plus au long, pourquoi le démon et ses mauvais anges apprirent, autrefois, aux femmes l'art de se farder et les moyens d'embellir leurs corps. Ils volurent, sans doute, dit il, les récompenser des faveurs qu'elles leurs avaient accordés: Tertullien suppose donc qu'il y avait eu un mauvais commerce entre les mauvais anges et les femmes.

"Ce paradox n'est pas particulier à Tertullien, que plusieurs autres pères de l'Eglise devant et après lui ne l'aient pas avancé.

" Mais cette erreur a été solidement réfutée par St. Chrisostome, St. Augustin, St. Epiphane, etc.

"A l'occasion de cet étrange commerce, notre auteur fait une réflection qui passe les bornes de la raillerie. Les démons, dit il, sont vénus trouver les filles des hommes: tout démons qu'ils sont, ils en ont été favorablement reçu; il ne manquait que cette ignominie aux femmes, ut hæc ignominia fœminæ accedat. Nam cum et materias quasdam bene occultas et artes plurasque non bene revelatas, seculo, multo magis imperito prodidissent (siquidem et metallorum opera nudaverant et herbarum ingenia traduxerant et incantationum vires promulgaverant et omnem curiositatem usque ad stellarum interpretationem designaverant) proprie et quasi pesunt ariter fœminis instrumentum istud muliebris gloriæ contulerunt; lumina lapillorum, quibus brachia arctantur; et medicamenta ex fuco, quibus lanæ colorantur et illum ipsum nigrem pulverem, quo oculorum exordia producantur."

The above extract is from a French translation, or rather compendium, of Tertullian, which was sent me by M. Van Praët from the Bibliothèque du Roi at Paris. But, as many of the most curious passages were entirely omitted, the same gentleman was so obliging as to look for the Latin folio containing that very amusing article of Tertullian entitled "De Habitu Muliebri;" from which I had intended to have given in this note a longer extract, written out for me by Baron Joseph de Palm, from whose very beautiful German verses two inadequate translations will appear in this volume. The extract, however, was accidentally left at Paris; and, Zóphiël being reviewed and arranged for the last time at Keswick (England), I fear it may not reach me soon enough to be inserted.

PAGE 52, VERSE 4.

"With wreaths of gems, or made or found by him,
Or his enamoured brothers, when they bore
Love for the like."

This passage, like the preceding one, is simply in pursuance of the belief of Tertullian, that the custom of arraying themselves with gold and gems was first taught to beautiful women by their angel lovers, who understood chemistry, and imparted to them, among other ornamental arts, that of preparing colors for dyeing their garments, and heightening the beauty of their complexions. But the sage Comte de Gabalis says that *gnomes* are the guardians of minerals and precious stones. I know not what origin he ascribes to his "peuples des elémens;" but he expressly affirms that no sylph or sylphide, gnome or gnômide, can be immortal unless united with a son or daughter of earth. Those who have any curiosity to know more must, I suppose, consult those learned authors whom he names in the following passage: —

"En croyez vous, dit il, plus à votre nourice qu'à la raison naturelle qu'à Platon, Pythagore, Celse, Psellus, Procle, Porphyre, Plotin, Trismegiste, Nolius, Dornée, Fludd; qu'au grand Philippe Aureole Theophraste Bombast Paracelse de Hohenheim, et qu'à tous nos compagnons?"

After describing the people of earth, air, fire, and water, the sage continues: "Il y avait beaucoup de proportion entre Adam et ces créatures si parfaites; parce qu'étant composé de ce qu'il y avait de plus pur dans les quatre élémens il renfermait les perfections de ces quatre espèces de peuples, et était leur roi naturel. Mais dès-lors que son péché l'eût précipité dans les particles les plus viles des élémens, comme vous verrez quelquefois, l'harmonie fut déconcertée, et il (Adam) n'eût plus de proportion, étant impur et grosier avec ces substances si purs et si subtiles."

PAGE 54, VERSE 3, LAST LINE.

"Slight bandelets were twined of colors five."

There is a German work by Hartmann on the toilet of Hebrew women, which those who are curious on the subject may do well to consult.

The father Calmet has also written a dissertation on the dress of the ancient Hebrews, which the French translator of Tertullian says, "ne prouve pas clairement sa proposition." M. de Châteaubriand introduces his Cymodocée (when arrayed for a religious ceremony, after her conversion to Christianity) in the same costume chosen by Egla for the banquet of Sardius.

Page 55, Verse 3.

This description is from the life, and does not exceed in any particular the *face* of a Canadian lady of Swiss descent. She was called by the peasants of her neighborhood "l'ange des bois."

Page 59, Verse 2, Line 1.

It is said by Pliny that Appion raised up the soul of Homer in order to learn from him his country and his parents, and Apollonius Tyanæus is said to have raised the manes of Achilles.

Page 59, Verse 4.

"*And oft his mother, vain in her delight,*
Boasted she owed him to a god's embrace."

The Christian fathers did not in the least doubt that many of the heroes of antiquity were really so produced. They, however, supposed that their fathers were some of the banished angels, who assumed at pleasure the forms of those gods under whose names they caused themselves to be adored.

Page 61, Verse 4.

"*Not Eva, lovelier than the tints of air.*"

The beauty which the antediluvian women must have possessed, in order to be such a temptation to angels as the Christian fathers supposed them to have been, agrees with the account of "Rabadan the Morisco," whose poem is said by Dr. Southey to contain "the fullest Mohammedan Genesis."

The Creator, having formed the earth, and adjusted his plan of procedure, summoned his angels, and requested that one of them might descend, and bring him soil or clay wherewith to make a man; but the angels unanimously expressed a reluctance to what they could but consider a loathsome and debasing office. Azaraël, however, an *angel of extraordinary stature*, flew down, and collected the material required from the north, east, south, and west of the new-made earth. "Azaraël," said the Creator, "thou shalt, in reward of thine obedience, be him who separateth the souls from the bodies of the creatures I am about to make: henceforth be called Azaraël Malec el Mout, or Azaraël the Angel of Death."

The Creator then caused the earth which Azaraël had brought to be washed and purified in the fountains of heaven, till it became so resplendently clear, that it cast a more shining and beautiful light than the sun in its utmost glory. Gabriel was then commanded to carry this lovely though as yet inanimate statue of clay throughout the heavens, the earth, *the centres*, and the seas.

When the angels saw so beautiful an image, they said, "Lord, if it be pleasing in thy sight, we will, in thy most high and mighty name, prostrate ourselves before it." This proposal meeting the approbation of the Creator, the angels all bowed, inclining their celestial countenances at the feet of the inanimate Adam.

Eblis, or Lucifer, was the only one who refused, proudly valuing himself upon his heavenly composition: whereupon the Creator said to him, with extreme sternness, "Prostrate thyself to Adam." He made a show of doing so, but remained upon his knees, and then rose up before he had performed what God had commanded him.

The other angels, seeing him so refractory, prostrated themselves a second time in order to complete what he had left undone. For this reason the Mohammedans, in all their prayers, at each inclination of the body, make two prostrations, one immediately after the other. — *See Rabadan.*

Page 61, Verse 4, Line 3.

"That form, all panting 'neath her yellow hair."

Milton has described the hair of the first woman as of a yellow or golden tint. This color appears to have been admired from the most remote antiquity. Indeed, when fine eyes, and symmetry of outline, are united with a white, transparent skin, and hair of this color in profusion, the form so constructed and adorned seems more than mortal. Persons of this complexion are generally of tender, voluptuous dispositions, and not naturally addicted to the passions of hatred and revenge. Such, however, are extremely rare, and, unless by the race of artists, seem, at present, less appreciated than beauties of a darker shade. Black hair and eyes embellish very much a common face and person; and, could one look entirely over the world, the aggregate of comeliness would perhaps be found greater among the dark than among the fair haired nations.

The Athenian ladies, so late as the time of Alcibiades, wore a yellow powder in their hair to give it the appearance of gold.

Josephus writes that King Solomon caused many of the finest horses of those presented him by neighboring princes to be ridden by young men, chosen at the most beautiful period of their lives, and remarkable for stature, and symmetry of person. These, dressed in the rich colors of Tyre, wore their hair long, and sprinkled with golden dust. This king, so renowned for his wisdom, deserves to be still more so for his taste. The murder of his brother, as related by Josephus, however, though so little mentioned, is a very dark blot on his character. Pleasure is too generally selfish and cruel.

PAGE 63, VERSE I.

"*And round his neck an amulet he wore*
Of many a gem in mystic mazes tied."

Men of all countries and ages have put faith in these talismans. The Egyptians have left a great number: they wore them on the neck, in the form of little cylinders, ornamented with figures and hieroglyphics.

"Les Grecs faisaient aussi un grand usage des amulettes; ils attribuerent des propriétés surnaturelles au laurier, au saule, aux arbrisseaux épineux, au jaspe, à presque toutes les pierres précieuses." — *Voyages d'Antenor.*

"The Arabs," says Shaw, "hang about their children's necks the figure of an open hand, which the Turks and Moors paint upon their ships and houses, as an antidote and counter-charm to an evil eye. Those who are grown up still carry about with them some paragraph or other of their Koran, which, as the Jews did their phylacteries, they place upon their breast, or sew under their caps, to prevent fascination and witchcraft, and to secure themselves from sickness and misfortune. The virtue of these charms and scrolls is supposed likewise to be so far universal, that they suspend them upon the necks of their cattle, horses, and other beasts of burden."

The most wonderful properties were ascribed to precious stones: some detected the presence of poison; others made ineffectual the power of evil spirits and magicians.

"Giafar, the founder of the Barmecides, being obliged to fly from Persia, his native country, took refuge at Damascus, and implored the protection of the caliph Soliman. When he was presented to that prince, the caliph suddenly changed color, and commanded him to retire, suspecting he had poison about him. Soliman had discovered it by means of *ten stones* which he wore upon his arm. They were fastened there like a bracelet, and never failed to strike against each other, and make a slight noise, when any poison was near. Upon inquiry, it was found that Giafar carried poison in his ring, for the purpose of self-destruction in case he had been taken by his enemies." — *Marigny.*

Sir Walter Scott avails himself very beautifully of that power of detecting poison attributed to the opal.

Belief in the efficacy of amulets is too pleasing to be easily laid aside; and probably will, in some degree, exist as long as the pain of fear or the pleasure of security. I was shown last evening, in company with a young Greek of Athens, an amulet which had belonged to his deceased companion. It was a little square case of silver, suspended from a chain, in order to be worn about the neck in the manner of a miniature. On the outside were three small figures in relief, — the Saviour, Mary, and Martha; and the case contained a thin slip of light-colored wood, about an inch in breadth, and an inch and a half in length, delicately carved, and representing a figure on horseback. This wood was supposed, by its former possessor, to be a fragment of the real cross. The Greek youth in whose presence it was shown has been educated by a gentleman of the south of England, and now living at the foot of Skiddaw with his enchanting lady. The protectors are all generosity, the youth all gratitude; and nothing can be more interesting than their family circle. The latter recollected some of the airs of his native country, which were wild and sweet, and, accompanied by the piano-forte, had a fine effect; and it was difficult to forbear thinking of those lyres which once might possibly have thrilled to them.

KESWICK, April 19, 1831.

PAGE 66, VERSE 2, LAST LINE.

"By magic skill, some philtre with his wine."

The ancients were much addicted to this practice, and sometimes died in consequence of mixtures secretly thrown into their drink or food for the purpose of securing their love for particular persons. A pretty incident of the kind is introduced into that very entertaining work, "Les Voyages d'Antenor." According to Josephus, the immediate cause of the execution of Mariamne was Herod's fear of such experiments. Sending for this queen in a violent fit of fondness, he met nothing but coldness and reproaches in return; and, while stung to the soul at her behavior, his mother and sister took the opportunity to inform him that Mariamne had prepared for him a love-potion.

PAGE 66, VERSE 3, LINE 1.

"Or there's in her blue eye some wicked light."

The fear of hurtful influences emanating from the eyes of persons suspected of magic was common to most nations of antiquity, and perhaps is not yet entirely laid aside in some parts of Europe.

"Les Thessaliens, les Illyriens, et les Triballes, étaient célèbre par leurs enchantemens. Les derniers, selon Pline, pouvaient faire périr des animaux et des enfans par leurs seule regards.

"Les anciens craignaient les regards des envieux autant pour eux-mêmes que pour leurs enfans; c'est pourquoi ils attachaient les mêmes amulettes au cou de leurs enfans: ils en mettaient aux jambes des portes, de manière qu'en les ouvrant on agitait ces phallus, et on ébranlait les clochettes." — *Voyages d'Antenor.*

Page 68, Verse 2, Last Line.

"*And twines her long hair round him as he sings.*"

This act was often resorted to as the most forcible manner of imploring protection. When the young prince Cyrus was brought before his brother Artaxerxes, whose throne he had attempted to usurp, Parysates, his mother, intwined him with her hair, and by tears and entreaties succeeded in saving him from death.

Page 70, Verse 4.

"*He died of love, — of the o'er-perfect joy*
Of being pitied, prayed for, prest by thee!"

Zimmermann, in his admired work on Solitude, gives an instance of two Italian lovers, who, after having been separated, sprang into each other's embrace, and both died immediately. Joy is seldom perfect enough to kill; but, could it exist as free from the alloy of any other sensation as grief is sometimes felt, it would probably destroy life much sooner, from the circumstance of mortal nerves being far less accustomed to it. "Many," said Dr. Goldsmith, "die of grief; but who was ever known to die of joy?" Instances of the latter, though rare, are sometimes found.

I was told by a lady, whose word there was not the least reason to doubt, of a person she had known who was passionately fond of music. She had heard him say, while listening to a concert of sacred compositions, "I shall certainly die if I hear many more of these strains." A few years afterwards, the same person actually fell dead while assisting at a concert. This happened in a country where education and every custom tend rather to the annihilation than the culture of any deep or violent emotion.

PAGE 72, VERSE 2, LAST LINE.

"*But gained a bliss frail nature could not bear.*"

Excessive joy, by preventing sleep (as it invariably does in a person capable of feeling it at all), very soon procures for itself a mitigation proceeding from corporeal uneasiness: were this not the case, it would soon terminate in death or madness, even though not felt in a very unusual degree.

Past joy is a thing so pleasant to speak upon, that raptures are generally exaggerated in the telling. When really intense, as they are sometimes described, their power to produce death can scarcely be doubted. Every one has heard of Chilo's death in the arms of his son, who returned victorious from the Olympic games.

PAGE 72, VERSES 4 AND 5.

"*It is whispered that the Unquelled desires*
Another Spirit for each forfeit seat
Left vacant by our fall."

It was an idea generally entertained by the fathers, that the many vacancies caused by the different orders of angels who fell through love or ambition were to be filled up by souls selected from the human species. Another opinion afterwards arose, and was favored by one or more of the popes, "that it was only the tenth order of the celestial hierarchy which supplied angels, who, by falling, assimilated themselves to the inhabitants of earth; and that it is only to supply the deficiencies of that grade that the best of mortals will be promoted." Much interesting speculation on this subject may be found in the works of Dionysius, to which I had free access while at Paris, but no time to make extracts or translations.

Page 74, Verses 3 and 4.

The Assyrians, Persians, and Medians are said not to have burned their dead; but the mother of Altheëtor was an Ionian, — the only reason that can be assigned for Zóphiël's supposing he would be burnt after the Grecian manner.

Page 74, Verse 5.

" O my loved Hyacinth! when as a god
I hurled the disk, and from thy hapless head
The pure sweet blood made flowers upon the sod."

This, and other passages which serve to identify Zóphiël with Apollo, are perfectly conformable to a belief *once* acknowledged by every Christian.

An able writer in "The North-American Review" (in an article entitled "Ancient and Modern Poetry," which appeared some time between the years twenty-one and four) appears to have read a great deal on the subject. The following is not irrelative: "Some evil spirits or fallen angels, whom the fathers had cast out, were compelled by the fire of exorcism to confess that they were the same who had inspired the heathen poets; and these, with all the duties of 'gay religions full of pomp and gold,' were confined to the doom of that infernal host described by Milton. So far were the Christians from denying the existence of any of the beings of Pagan mythology, that they continually urged, as an argument in favor of the superiority and divinity of their faith, the power which it gave over them; and Eunapius (see Eunapius' life of Porphyry in his Vitæ Philosophorum) very gravely mentions the story of Porphyry's expelling a demon."

M. de Fontenelle wrote his "Histoire des Oracles" expressly to prove that heathen temples were not inhabited by demons or fallen angels. In that work is found the following oracle, extracted from the writings of Eusebius: "Unhappy priest," said Apollo to one of his ministers, "ask me no more concerning the Divine Father, nor of his only Son, nor of that Spirit which is the soul of all things: it is that Spirit which expels me forever from these abodes."

Page 74, Last Verse, Line 1.

See fable of Zephyr and Hyacinth. Oriel is supposed to show himself to mortals as Zephyrus, while Phraërion in reality nurses and protects the flowers.

Page 75, Verse 3, Last Line.

Zóphiël, as may be perceived, since his first introduction, is supposed to be that fallen angel who was adored by mortals as the god Apollo. This manner of imparting to a young artist excellence in sculpture is not, therefore, out of character.

Page 77, Last Verse.

" Dejected Egla went
With all her house, and seeks her own acacia-grove."

The facility with which the young king of Media forgets his beautiful captive, setting aside the effect produced by the premature death of Altheëtor his preserver, agrees perfectly with the following description: —

"Nous rencontrames une troupe à cheval leste et brillant, à la tête de laquelle était le jeune Pharnabaze, l'air serein et radieux, faisant caracoler son cheval, et plaisantant avec ses camarades; j'en fus étourdis: je l'avais vue, la veille, desespéré; s'arrachant les cheveux, se jettant sur le corps de la belle Statira; invoquant la mort, voulant se poignarder; et, déjà, la rire, le plaisir, avait succédés à ce grand désespoir." — *Voyages d'Antenor.*

NOTES TO CANTO THIRD.

PALACE OF GNOMES.

Having liberty, while at Paris, to take any books I might wish from the Bibliothèque du Roi, and M. Van Praët being very obliging in looking for them, it was in my power to make much more copious notes than will appear to this canto, which, from its subject, admits of a great variety. Many obstacles and engagements occurred to prevent; which I regret only because many passages of the old Christian writers and their Pagan contemporaries, on the subject of angels and other spirits, are extremely curious and entertaining. Sufficient poetical authority is, however, given for the incidents of the story; and the text, perhaps, is sufficiently explained. Copious notes extracted from the works of others indicate nothing but toil and patience in the writer.

PAGE 81, VERSE 2, LINE 1.

"*The heavenly angel watched his subject star.*"

This line is in accordance with the belief that the stars are guarded by celestial intelligences, to the prevalence of which many passages in the sacred writings bear testimony, and from which may be inferred a possibility that each inhabited and separate planet may, in reality, be under the care of some delegate spirit. Saturnius of Antioch taught that "the world and its first inhabitants were created by seven angels, which presided over the seven planets;" and that "the work was carried on without the knowledge of the *benevolent deity*, and in opposition to the material principle. The former, however, beheld it with approbation, and honored it with several marks of his beneficence."

Many singular systems of this kind are classed under the name of heresies by Mosheim.

PAGE 81, VERSE 3, LINE 3.

The trunk of the palm-tree is of a light dove or ash color, and assumes a silvery appearance by moonlight.

PAGE 82, VERSE 1, LINE 3.

"Myrrh her tears of fragrance weeps."

I had hoped to see the plant myrrh in the Jardin des Plantes at Paris, but was disappointed. Its appearance, however, can be easily conceived by the following: "Mr. Bruce, while in Abyssinia, made some remarks on the myrrh-tree, which are to be found in the 'Journal de Physique,' &c., tome xiii., 1778. He (Bruce) says that the naked troglodytes brought him specimens of myrrh, of which both the leaves and bark bore a great resemblance to the *acacia vera*." Among the leaves he observed some straight prickles about two inches in length. He likewise mentions seeing a *saffa-tree*, which was a native of the myrrh country, covered with beautiful crimson flowers. Drops of perfume distil from this tree, which probably harden into that substance called myrrh, which is common in medicine. In one of the letters of M. Demonstier's delightful work on Mythology the young Adonis is represented as pointing to a myrrh-tree, and exclaiming, "Hélas! ces larmes précieuses sont les pleurs de ma mère!" who, according to the fable, was metamorphosed by the gods in compassion to her grief.

PAGE 82, VERSE 1, LAST LINE.

For an account of the "spikenard of the ancients," Sir William Jones may be referred to with pleasure. One species of it is said to have been discovered by the horses and elephants of the vizier Afufaddaulah. "If the spikenard of India was a reed, or grass, we can never be able to discover it among the genera of those natural orders which here form a wilderness of sweets; and some of them have not only fragrant roots, but even *spikes*, in the ancient and modern sense of that emphatical word."

PAGE 82, VERSE 2, LINE 1.

"Proud prickly cerea, now thy blossom 'scapes
Its cell."

Few persons have seen the blossom of this astonishing flower, because it only opens at or after midnight, and is so evanescent, that, unless constantly watched, it is difficult to know the exact time of its perfection. It is large, and of a yellowish white; and in its cup, or rather in the midst of its fragrant petals, there is an appearance of lambent light or flame, resembling burning nitre.

PAGE 82, VERSE 3, LINE 3.

The ancients throughout Syria (though ignorant of some useful principles discovered by modern science) were very skilful in hydraulics. Some of the earlier kings of that country had gardens with fountains and artificial streams without the walls of Jerusalem, in a place which is now a parched and barren desert.—*See Josephus.*

PAGE 82, LAST VERSE, LAST LINE.

Of all the varieties of this celebrated flower, the red or rose-colored is the most admired for its fragrance; the white and yellow give a fainter odor; and the azure-colored lotos, which is a native of Persia and Cashmir, is perhaps the most beautiful of all.

Page 83, Verse 2, Line 1.

The night-blooming cereus is fond of clasping rocks, old walls, or fallen trees. It grows in profusion where these verses were written (Cuba), and produces a fruit not unpleasant to the taste.

Page 86, Verse 4, Last Lines.

" To share its joys, assist its vast design
With high intelligence: oh dangerous gift!"

It is said that the angels who rebelled were among the most wise and powerful of celestial creatures. None of them were more resplendent in beauty than Lucifer, who drew with him, when he fell, a third part of the stars of heaven.

The supposition that many beings, subordinate to the supreme will, were employed in that disposition of matter called "the creation," is not only according to every system of religion, but agreeable to all analogy. "God said, Let there be light; and light was." The King of Persia commanded a temple to be built, and it rose. There is little more reason to believe that the first was accomplished without multiplied means and agency than the last. Every thing in natural history and in natural philosophy favors the idea of an infinity of beings to supply the gradations between man and the Sovereign of creation. Indeed, after thinking a little on the subject, it seems almost absurd to believe the contrary. This belief, besides, is far more pleasing in itself than that of regarding the Supreme Giver of life only as an all-competent artisan.

M. l'Abbé Poule, discoursing upon a future state of existence, gives the following passage:—

"Ils ne seront plus cachés, pour nous, ces êtres innombrables, qui échappent à nos connoissances par leur éloignement ou par leur petitesse; les différentes parties qui composent le vaste ensemble de l'univers; leurs structures, leur rapport, leur harmonie; ils ne seront plus des énigmes, pour nous, ces jeux surprenans, ces secrets profonds de la nature, ces ressorts admirables que la providence emploie pour la conservation et la propagation de tous les êtres."

I translate from the French of M. de Châteaubriand the following delightful passage: "The sovereign happiness of the elect is a consciousness that their joys are never to be terminated. They are incessantly in the same delicious state of mind as a mortal who has just performed a good or heroic action, a man of genius who has just given birth to a sublime conception, of a person in the first transports of an unforbidden love, or the charms of a friendship made certain by a long series of adversity. The nobler passions are not extinguished by death, in the hearts of the just; and whenever they are found, even on earth, respire something of the grandeur and eternity of the Supreme Intelligence."

Page 87, Verse 4, Last Line.

From the blooming of the roses at Ecbatana to the coming-in of spices at Babylon.

Page 88, Verse 4, Last Line, and Verse 5.

" *That vague, wondrous lore*

" *But seldom told to mortals,—arts on gems*
Inscribed that still exist; but hidden so,
From fear of those who told, that diadems
Have passed from brows that vainly ached to know."

It is said to have been believed by the Egyptians that many *wonderful secrets* were engraved by one of the Mercuries on tablets of emerald, which still remain hidden in some part of their country.

Being assisted by a friend in looking over the first part of Brucker's "Historia Critica Philosophiæ" for something concerning these tablets of emerald, we were soon disappointed by the following passage:—

"Non detenibimus itaque lectorem fabularum de Mercurio Græcarum atque Latinarum recitatione, quas qui legere vult, apud Lilium Gyraldum (Lugd. Bat. 1698, 4) vel Natalem Comitem (Mythol. L. V., c. 5. P. M. 439) aliosque mythologiæ veteris interpretes abunde inveniet unde sitem extinguat." To those authors, therefore, the reader is referred.

Some of the fathers (Tertullian in particular) supposed that all impious and daring sciences, such as magic and alchemy, came to the heathen nations through the medium of fallen angels, who, during the violence of their love for particular women, would sometimes reveal to them doctrines and truths which could never otherwise have been conceived by their poets and philosophers.

Petrarch, in a letter to Robert, King of Naples, says, "The expectation which our faith presents was unknown to the heathen philosophers; but they felt that the soul was not to die." Pherecydes was the first among them who openly maintained it. Pherecydes most probably conceived his belief from *old and vague* traditions, confirmed by his own feelings and experience.

"Epicurus," continues Petrarch, "was the only one who denied it. From Pherecydes it passed to Pythagoras, from Pythagoras to Socrates, from Socrates to Plato; and Cicero established this doctrine in his discourses on friendship, old age, and other parts of his works."

The lives of all these philosophers, that of Socrates in particular, rather confirm than disprove the belief of the fathers respecting communications from a higher order of beings.

Page 92, Verse 3, Last Line.

"Though like thin shades or air they mock dull mortals' sight."

The discoveries effected by chemistry and natural philosophy, although they make apparent the fallacy of many superstitions, do not in the least disprove the existence of spiritual creatures. After hearing explained the nature of light and heat, and observing the effects produced by many common experiments, it is not difficult to conceive of beings powerful, beautiful, and exquisitely organized, yet of a material so refined and subtle as easily to elude the most perfect animal perception.

PAGE 92, VERSE 5, FIRST LINES.

"*The Palace of the Gnome,*
Tahathyam."

In respect to the birth of Tahathyam and his court, I have followed the opinion of Tertullian and others. The beings, however, which are described in the text, *can* only be called *gnomes* from their residence in the earth, and their knowledge of mineralogy and gems. The

"Four dusky spirits, by a secret art,
Taught by a father thoughtful of his wants,"

which "Tahathyam kept" in his immediate service, might have answered the description of the Comte de Gabalis.

"La terre est remplie, presque jusqu'au centre, de *gnomes*, gens de petites statures, gardiens des trésors, des minéraux, et des pierreries. Ceux-ci sont ingénieux, amis de l'homme, et faciles à commander. Les *gnomides*, leurs femmes, sont petites mais fort agréa bles et leur habit est fort curieux."

"Les gnomes et les sylphes sont mortels, mais cessent d'être mortel du moment qu'ils épousent une de nos filles."

"*De la naquit* l'erreur des premiers siècles, de Tertullien, du martyr Justin, de Lactance, de Cyprien, de Clement d'Alexandrie, d'Anathagore, philosophe Chrétien, *et généralement de tous les écrivains de ce tems là*. Ils avaient appris que ces *demi-hommes élémentaires* avaient recherché le commerce des filles; *et ils ont imaginé que la chute des anges n'étoit venue que de l'amour* dont ils s'étaient laissés toucher pour les femmes. Quelques *gnomes* désireux de devenir immortels avaient voulu gagner les bonnes graces de nos filles, et leur avaient apportées des pierreries dont ils sont gardiens naturels; et ces auteurs ont crû s'appuyans sur le livre d'Enoch mal-entendu, que c'étaient des pièges que les anges amoureux avaient préparés pour mieux en assurer la conquête." — *Comte de Gabalis.*

Though not immediately relative to the subject, I cannot forbear inserting the following curious account of sylphs · —

"L'air est plein d'une innombrable multitude de peuples de figure humaine, un peu fiers en apparence, mais dociles en effet: officieux aux sages, et ennemies des sots et des ignorans. Leurs femmes et leurs filles sont des beautés mâles telles qu'on depeint les amazones." — *Le même.*

PAGE 94, VERSE 4, LAST LINE.

Not far from the scene of Vulcan's labors: yet the regions sought by these spirits must have been very much deeper.

PAGE 99, VERSE 4.

" Had lightly left his pure and blissful home
To taste the blandishments of mortal love."

In the Book of Enoch, two hundred or more of such angels as Cephroniel are said to have descended on Mount Hermon for the purpose of visiting women of whose beauty they had become enamoured. Tertullian regards this book as of sacred authority, as will be seen in the article, " De Habitu Muliebri ; " but some of the other fathers are disinclined to believe it.

PAGE 100, VERSE 1.

This manner of bearing the car is not inconsistent with the known docility and strength of serpents in general.

PAGE 100, VERSE 2, LAST LINE.

Tsaveven signifies tint-gem.

PAGE 100, VERSE 3, LINE 2.

It has been said that an art once existed of composing a substance, which, together with a perfect pliancy, had the color and transparency of glass or crystal.

PAGE 100, VERSE 4.

"*The reptiles, in their fearful beauty, drew,*
As if from love, like steeds of Araby:
Like blood of lady's lip their scarlet hue."

The docility, and even affection, of the serpent, is sufficiently known and attested. Some chemical arts might have been used to give the scales of these their scarlet color, surrounded as they were by beings of such exquisite skill. Little serpents, however, of a bright glossy scarlet, are not uncommon in America; and (if the Count de Buffon, and his admirer and frequent translator Dr. Goldsmith, are to be relied on) the snake, as long as it lives, continues to increase, having no fixed dimensions allotted to it like other animals. These most pleasing writers (if I am not much mistaken) believe also that no particular bound is set to its vitality, and that it is capable of retaining life and youth so long as it can be preserved from accidents.

The following account of the celebrated exploit of Prometheus, which M. de Lentier puts into the mouth of an old Grecian or Assyrian mariner, may not be unentertaining:—

Prometheus, having made a statue of clay, mixed with it levin of gall, flesh of the aspic, and foam of the lion. But the figure was still an insensible mass. Prometheus stole fire from the sun, and man was animated. Scarcely had he drawn a breath ere he complained to the gods of the fatal gift of life: pain was his first sensation. Jupiter, to console him, and mitigate his sufferings, gave him a drug that had the virtue of restoring youth. The man was delighted with the present, and placed it on an ass for the purpose of conveying it to his own abode.

The beast, tormented with thirst, stopped on his way at a fountain guarded by a serpent. The wicked reptile would not suffer him to drink, except on condition that the drug should meanwhile be left in its care. The ass consented, and the serpent kept the drug. From that time the serpent has had power to renew its youth, while poor human beings grow old without remedy.

Page 101, Verse 3.

"Bright Ramaöur followed on, in order meet;
Then Nahalcoul and Zotzaraven, best
Beloved, save Rouämasak of perfume sweet;
Then Talhazak and Marmorak."

These names are formed from Hebraic words, expressive of the various qualities and employments of the beings who bear them.

Aishalat signifies fire-control; Psaämayim, black-water; Ramaöur, light-direct; Nahalcoul, guide-sound; Zotzaraven, shape-spar; Rouämasak, mingle-air; Talhazak, dew-congeal; Marmorak (partly Greek), marble-stain.

Nothing can be more barbarous than Hebrew words as they are pronounced in English. They are, however, much softer on the lips of Oriental speakers, or even those of the south of Europe. Some of the dialects of the aborigines of America, though they look so repulsively as we get them on paper, are soft as the murmur of the forest when spoken by forest orators.

Page 102, Verse 4.

Diamond, it is said, is but crystal of carbon. Tahathyam, however, might not have meant to have his flowers literally covered or incrusted with diamond, but might only have used this expression to impress on Talhazak a sense of the value he held them in.

Page 104, Verse 4.

"Where is the bright Cephroniel? Spirit, tell
But how he fares."

Tahathyam has never seen his father since first established in his submarine kingdom; and knows not whether he has been received again into heaven, or remains still wandering about in a state of punishment. The crimes of those angels made guilty only by their intercourse with mortals were supposed to have been punished less severely than those of the subordinates of the prince of ambition.

Page 105, Last Verse.

It was perfectly in the power of optics and chemistry, of which sciences these beings were in possession, to produce the effect described beneath the roof of so vast a cavern.

Page 107, Verse 4.

> " *That baffling, maddening, fascinating art,*
> *Half told by Sprite most mischievous, that he*
> *Might laugh to see men toil, then not impart.*"

Some alchemists still exist who have not laid aside the hope of success in their labors.

In Voltaire's "Life of Charles XII." is related the following circumstance: "A certain Livonian, who was an officer in the Saxon army, and named Paikel, was made prisoner by the troops of Charles, and condemned to be decapitated at Stockholm. Before the execution of his sentence he found means to inform the senate that he was in possession of the secret of making gold; which, on condition of pardon, he would communicate to the king. The experiment was made in prison, in presence of Col. Hamilton and the magistrates of the city. The gold found in the crucible after the experiment was carried to the mint at Stockholm, and a judicial report made to the senate; which appeared so important, that the queen-mother ordered the execution to be suspended until the king could be informed of so singular an event, and transmit his orders to Stockholm. Charles answered that he had refused the pardon of the criminal to his relations, and that he would never grant to interest what he had refused to friendship. After viewing the fable of Midas, *in connection with the belief of the fathers*, it is not difficult to imagine that the secret of alchemy was actually imparted to that king by a fallen angel, who caused himself to be adored as the god Bacchus; and the disastrous consequences that must necessarily ensue, provided such an art could be obtained, are forcibly depicted in the sufferings of Midas.

Gold, like every thing else not absolutely necessary to existence, would cease to be valued as soon as it became plentiful; but nothing would, perhaps, occasion more dreadful immediate misery than a possibility of procuring it easily.

The secret of alchemy, even if it could be discovered, would bring with it nothing delightful; but it is pleasant to imagine a glimpse of possibility of discovering, sooner or later, the means of preserving mortal life beyond its present imperfect term.

It has always seemed to me (whether any other person has thought the same I know not) that something in favor of this possibility may be inferred from a passage in the Mosaic account of the fall. The first pair are driven from the garden, lest, having *tasted* the tree of *knowledge*, they might pluck also of the tree of life, and *live forever.* Is this an allegory? or to what does the passage relate?

"The animals," says Father Jerom Dandini in his "Voyage to Mount Libanus," "eat a certain herb which causes their teeth to change to a golden color." This herb Father Jerom thinks must proceed from mines under Mount Ida. And Niebuhr mentions that the Eastern alchemists fancy their success would be certain, provided they could find out the herb which tinges the color of the flesh of the sheep that eat it.

PAGE 109, LAST VERSE; PAGE 110, VERSE 1.

"*In form of canopy was seen to fall*
The stony tapestry."

There now exists, either in Virginia or some of the neighboring country (I have no reference, and do not recollect this particular), a singularly beautiful grotto, called, by those who live around it, *Wyer's Cave.* It contains several apartments, in some of which the concretions are said by those who have seen them to be spread over the sides and roof in the form of curtains and festoons. One of the chambers is extremely remarkable. It is commonly called the "Lady's Drawing-room;" and on one side of it a crystalline projection is shown, which rings at the touch in such a manner, that the person whose description I saw fancied a skilful hand might draw music from it. Many curious and extensive caverns are found in the Island of Cuba. One near the Bay of Matanzas is often visited by strangers; but nobody has ventured to penetrate far. I visited one twenty miles distant from this, and not far from the estate San Patricio, which contained three apartments and a reservoir of water. Being a great deal above the surface of the earth, on the side of a pleasant hill, it would not, in that climate, have been very uncomfortable as a residence. Some of the concretions had attained the shape of large and perfect columns; others were in the form of two acute pyramids or obelisks, — one depending from the roof, and the other rising from the floor. These were of a whitish color; but though evening came on, and we had two or three tapers, I could see nothing transparent or sparkling. This grotto is on either the Cafétal Teresa, or the one adjoining it: the boundaries of both were covered with wood. There is another, deeper in the earth, about six or seven English miles from Matanzas, on the estate of Octavius Mitchell, Esq., from which I was shown specimens of spar of the size and shape of a common quill, and clear like glass. Some beautiful concretions, or perhaps petrifactions, were also found there, which were said to bear some resemblance to groups of sculpture. These I did not see; but one was taken out, and named "The Twins of Latona."

PAGE 110, VERSE 4, LINE 3.

This name is compounded of a Hebraic and a Greek word, and signifies to move or affect the soul.

PAGE 114, LAST VERSE, FIRST WORDS.

From *eva*, life; and *nathan*, to give.

NOTES TO CANTO FOURTH.

THE STORM.

PAGE 119, VERSE 2, LAST LINE.

"And fed on the revenge deep smouldering in his breast."

Caius Marius, musing over the ruins of Carthage, has been made the subject of a very good picture; and the author of that not very old Italian work entitled "Notti Romane" has entered with great effect into those feelings which the successor of Sylla probably acted under. If the characters of those who commit crimes could be analyzed, it would be found, perhaps invariably, that such persons are either too stupid to be sensible of what they do, or under some illusion of feeling or imagination which entirely conceals from them its atrocity.

"Nodrito dalla sola vendetta m' inoltrai sulla spiaggia peregrinando verso Minturno: ivi mi abbattei immantininte ne' guerrieri Sillani miei indefessi persecutori. Mi gettai fra le onde a nuoto, e mi rivolei a due navi, non remote, per ricoverarmi in esse. Le gravi, provette, vaste, oppresse, mie membra faceano a stento quell' offizio, cosi che il sommergermi era imminente, lo udiva, intanto que' sicarj dal lido far voti crudeli a Nettuno, ed a Nereo perche mi traessero negli abbissi loro, et invocare i mostri voraci del mare; e schernire con ribalde parole quella mia trista ansietà.

'"A me sospinto da continue sciagure, scacciato da ogni lido, era omai divenuto ogni terra inospitale, ogni mare tempestoso; e stetti muto contemplando la ruine della spenta Cartagine, come specchio della fortuna." —*Notti Romane.*

Marius, soon after the scene depicted in this extract, returned to Rome, and (as he is made to express it in the same work) purged the city of its horrid ingratitude.

Page 119, Verse 3, Last Line.

"*From where with children's blood their guilty altars reek.*"

The Carthaginians retained the custom of offering human sacrifices to their gods till the destruction of their city. When Gelon of Syracuse gained a victory over them in Sicily, one of the articles of stipulation was that no more human lives should be sacrificed to Saturn. "For," says Rollin, "during the whole engagement, which lasted from morn till night, Hamilcar, the son of Hanno, was continually offering to the gods sacrifices of living men, who were thrown on a flaming pile." Seeing his troops put to flight, Hamilcar threw himself upon the same pile, and received, after his death, divine honors. Mothers (according to Plutarch and Tertullian) threw their children into the sacrificial flames, and the least indication of pity or sorrow would have been punished in them as impious.

According to the belief of the fathers, it must have been the princely instigator of the rebellion in heaven who caused himself to be adored as the god Belus or Saturn, whose altars were continually glowing with the blood and flames of human sacrifices. Those angels who fell from the thirst of power must have been the authors of all cruelty. The seraphic offenders were only voluptuous. The angel presiding over licentious love is sometimes forcibly alluded to in "Les Martyrs" of M. de Châteaubriand.

Page 119, Last Verse, First Lines.

"But far, far off, upon the sea's expanse,
The very silence has a shriek of fear."

In the suspense and stillness which precede a storm on or near the ocean, or any other vast extent of water, there is an effect produced on the feelings of some persons as if a shriek were really uttered in the distance. This effect was probably attributed, by such of the ancients as observed it, to their sea-gods or nymphs. Christian fathers or Jewish rabbins must have supposed it to proceed from those angels, who, according to the books of the latter, preside over the elements.

Page 124, Verse 1, Line 1.

"The shivering Sprite of flowers."

According to the Hebraic writings, nothing animate or inanimate exists throughout all nature without a particular angel to protect and take care of it.

"Archangelos et angelos, quibus cura committitur Regnorum, provinciarum, Nationum, principum, et particularium personarum; quæritur igitur, num etiam animalia bruta, et res insensibiles, id est lapides, et elementa atque etiam vegetabilia habeant proprios Angelos ad sui custodiam destinatos?"—*Bibliotheca Magna Rabbinica: Bartoloccii.*

This, whether true or false, is much more delightful than the belief or knowledge that every thing depends on material laws. The Greeks had a nymph for every tree; and their religion was a mere alteration of those of the more Oriental and ancient nations. The idea of the Elysian Fields was, it has been supposed, conceived by Orpheus after a glance at the vast subterranean abodes of the priests of Egypt, who, as is usual, converted those sublime truths conveyed to them, according to the faith of the fathers, by erring but celestial intelligences, to purposes of the grossest fraud and cruelty.

PAGE 125, LAST VERSE; PAGE 126, VERSE 1.

"Not, as 'tis wont, with intermitting flash,
But like an ocean all of liquid flame."

This is but a simple description of the appearance of the sky for several minutes during a storm which happened on the island where the verses of the text were written, either in the year 1823 or 1824. I lay under a transparent mosquito-net, listening to the pleasing noise made by the trees and shrubs around the principal dwelling of the Cafétal San Patricio, and watching the flashes of lightning that darted through the green blinds of an unglazed window. It was about midnight when the loudness of the thunder-peals increased, and the flashes became more continued than any I had ever seen. A crash was soon heard from without, and the whole room seemed deluged, as it were, with flame.

Thinking the building on fire, I arose, and succeeded in waking a negress, who still slept soundly by the door of my apartment. Going into the hall, and getting a window opened which looked into a broad piazza, I was surprised to see it occupied by those fierce dogs which were accustomed to be let loose at ten or eleven o'clock at night, in order that they might prowl about till sunrise, and guard the plantation. They had sought shelter from the elements: and, as they ran in a distressed manner from one side of the piazza to the other, it seemed as if they moved in fire; for the whole firmament continued to be, at long intervals, like a vast sea of light. Some glazed windows on the slant roof of the building were torn from their hinges, and whirled over the secaderos;[1] and the rain then descended in cataracts.

The sun rose brightly next morning; and the scene, though rather sad, was delightful. The Bermuda grass-plats were strewn with leaves, twigs, and broken flowers: and numbers of those black birds which the Spanish inhabitants of the island call *judeos* were hovering over a dark clump of bamboos which had been torn

[1] Secaderos are made of plaster, in the manner of broad platforms, rising a little, however, in the centre, and formed with many divisions and conduits for the rain, which is retained in cisterns beneath them. On these the red and sweet-smelling coffee-berries are dried.

up by the roots, and uttering the most piteous cries; for many of them were unable to find again their nests, constructed amidst the almost impervious foliage of those vast and beautiful reeds which now lay prostrate.

The palm thatching was torn from some of the out-houses of San Patricio. One mansion on a neighboring estate, belonging to Don José Martinez, was taken by the tempest from an insecure foundation, and set in another place. One estate, several leagues distant, and near a river, was deluged. But no human lives, that I heard of, were lost.

Page 127, Verse 3.

"A sable mantle fell in cloudy fold
From its stupendous breast."

That many of the angels were of a larger stature than that of men appears to have been believed by the Oriental nations. Asrael, or Azaraël, who assisted in forming the first man, was, according to Rabadan the Morisco, noticed particularly by the Creator on account of his uncommon stature.

Herodotus relates that Xerxes, while yet undecided upon carrying the war into Greece, was warmly dissuaded from his design by his brother Artabanes. Falling asleep soon after, he saw in a dream a man of uncommon stature and beauty, who urged him on to the undertaking. This, Calmet supposes, must have been some angel or spirit who sought his destruction.

It is said of Apollonius Tyaneus, that, coming to the tomb of Achilles, he raised his manes, and begged that the figure of the hero might appear to him: whereupon a phantom appeared like a young man, seven feet and a half high, which soon increased to twelve cubits, and assumed an extraordinary beauty. The whole, however, proved to be the work of a demon which Apollonius had power over. This incident is introduced by Byron in "The Deformed Transformed."

PAGE 129, VERSE 3.

"There, on the steam of human heart-blood, spilt
By priest or murderer, make repast."

Those evil spirits or angels who caused themselves to be adored as deities, were said to subsist (according to M. de Fontenelle, who gives authority for all that he asserts, "Leurs corps aëriens se nourissent de fumigations de sang répandu et de la graisse de sacrifices." — *Histoire des Oracles*) on the smoke of sacrifices. One is almost induced to believe, with the earlier Christians, that demons really inhabited those temples where so much human blood was spilled. It is far more shocking to suppose that so horrid an expedient could have been invented by one's fellow-mortals for the purposes of deception or interest.

PAGE 129, VERSE 3.

"Over the vile creations of thy guilt."

It is not impossible that some of the angels who assisted at the creation (as is believed by all very ançient nations) might, after the fall, have amused themselves with making those noisome and disgusting reptiles and animalcula which can but startle one's belief in the beneficence of the Being who formed them.

PAGE 129, VERSE 4.

"Waste thy life-giving power on reptiles foul."

Life, it is supposed, may exist without the slightest mixture of soul, as is the case with many marine animals. Some chemists, in the enthusiasm of their successes, have imagined that even human life was kept up by a mechanical process carried on in the lungs. This, granting it *for a moment* to be true, does not in the least detract from the power or bounty of the great Creator and Fountain of soul; for of what value is any animated form unless ennobled by a breath or emanation from him?

After receiving it as a truth, that such beings as good and evil angels exist, one may reasonably suppose them in possession of many arts and much science, which men, from the shortness of their lives, have been unable to attain.

PAGE 129, LAST VERSE.

" While, blent with winds, ten thousand agents wage
The strife anew."

Many passages in the writings of both Jews and Christians occur to justify this. It must, however, have been some inferior angel, who, according to the continually quoted belief of the fathers, was worshipped as the god Æolus. The "prince of the powers of the air" himself must have been sufficiently employed in feasting on the exhalations of the blood of his numerous sacrifices. The god Mars, to preserve the same system entire, must have been also one of his subordinates. The field of battle, therefore, together with the hearts that quivered on altars both in the Old and New World, must have made his banquets long and frequent.

PAGE 132, VERSE 4.

" Though the first seraph formed, how could I tell
The ways of guile?"

The angels are supposed to have been created at different periods: they were endowed with different capacities, and had different employments assigned to them.

"Cùm enim soli Angeli supremæ hierarchiæ immediaté illuminentur à Deo, illi soli dicuntur assistere Deo; cæteri aliarum hierarchiarum, ministrantes Angeli nominantùr. Itaque tam illi, quam isti sunt fere infiniti." — *Bibliotheca Magna Hebraica: Bartoloccii.*

NOTES TO CANTO FIFTH.

ZAMEÏA.

PAGE 138, VERSE 4, LINE 1.

"'*Tis there thou bid'st a deeper ardor glow.*"

It has been generally believed that "the cold in clime are cold in blood;" but this, on examination, would, I am convinced, be found *physically untrue*, at least, in those climates near the equator. It is here that most cold-blooded animals, such as the tortoise, the serpent, and various tribes of beautiful insects, are found in the greatest perfection.

Fewer instances of delirium or suicide, occasioned by the passion of love, would, perhaps, be found within the tropics than in the other divisions of the earth. Nature, in the colder regions, appears to have given an innate warmth and energy proportionate to those efforts which the severity of the elements, and the numerous wants which they create, keep continually in demand.

Those who live, as it were, under the immediate protection of the sun, have little need of internal fires. Their blood is cool and thin; and, living where every thing is soft and flattering to the senses, it is not surprising that their thoughts seldom wander far beyond what their bright eyes can look upon.

Though sometimes subject to violent fits of jealousy, these generally pass off without leaving much regret or unhappiness behind; and any other object falling in their way (for they would not go far to seek it) would very soon become just as valuable to them as the one lost. Such of them as are constant are rather so from indolence than from any depth of sentiment, or conviction of excellence. "The man who reflects," says Rousseau, "is a monster out of the order of nature." The natives of all tropical regions might be brought forward in proof of his assertion: they never look at remote results, or enter into refined speculations; and yet are, undoubtedly, less unhappy than any other of the inhabitants of earth.

Page 139, Verse 3, Last Line.

"*Excess of soul through the material breast.*"

I have never observed this effect except in very few instances, and those were of persons neither brilliant for their attainments, nor (with one exception) remarkable for external beauty. They were, however, possessed of most excellent dispositions; and it was impossible to converse with them without being sensible of something which could be felt, and almost seen, — a sort of emanation.

Page 139, Verse 4, Last Lines.

"*A warmth — a mystic charm — seemed breathing through*
Each viewless pore, and circling him without."

This is but a copy from the life, and the original of it was so uneducated as to be scarcely tolerable: he had made, however, the most generous sacrifices for his friends and relatives; and it was impossible to be near and look at him, while speaking, without perceiving all attempted to be described in the text.

Page 140, Verse 3, Last Line.

For the origin of the name of this mountain or ridge, see an article on Mount Caucasus in "Asiatic Researches."

Page 142, Verse 1, Last Line.

"Cast me to the flames, and save me from the thought!"

Human victims were sometimes thrown into fires burning in honor of the god Baal. It appears from some passages in the Mosaic writings that the same custom prevailed even among the Hebrews.

Page 142, Verse 4, Last Lines.

"Forsake
All other gods for love's idolatry."

It appears that the Hebrews were not averse to intermarrying with those of other nations, provided such would embrace their religion. "Pharaoh's daughter became, it is supposed, a proselyte: a marriage with her was not, therefore, considered a fault in their wise but voluptuous king." — *See Notes to Josephus.*

Page 145, Verse 4, Line 2.

The carneol is a gem of carnation tint, which for hardness ranks little below the ruby and amethyst.

Page 146, Last Verse, Last Line.

"Are thrown to bear you to some floating isle."

For an account of those flowery islets which once floated about the Mississippi, from whose mud and vegetation they were formed, one has only to look at the beginning of "Atala." There M. de Châteaubriand has given a description surpassed only by the exquisite story which follows.

The Mexicans, before the conquest of their city by Cortez, were accustomed to sail about its lakes on floating islets: these, however, must have been constructed by art.

PAGE 147, VERSE 1, LAST LINE.

"He rears his white-ringed neck, and watches you from far."

The ring-necked serpent is still sometimes seen in North America: it is of a shining black, with a white circle about its neck, as exact as if drawn with a pencil. From the extreme swiftness of its movement, it received from the English settlers the name of horse-racer. Its lifts its head, from time to time, above the grass through which it glides; and is said to have the power of destroying even men by twining itself about them. If death, however, has ever happened from that cause, the cases of it must have been very unfrequent. I saw, when a child, a very young snakelet of this kind, which had been found in a cellar, and was kept in spirits of wine by the woman of the house: it was of the length of a common pen, and very smooth and delicate.

PAGE 148, VERSE 1, LAST LINE.

"That from the City of the Dove ye came."

The dove was, in ancient times, the device of the Assyrian Empire, as the eagle was that of the Roman; and was adopted from a belief that the Indian god Mahá-dévá, and his goddess Párvaté, once assumed the appearance of doves in order to benefit the inhabitants.

The worship of the dove was peculiar to India, Arabia, Syria, and Assyria. Semiramis, the queen and beautifier of Babylon, is said to have been fed by doves in the desert, and to have vanished at last from the sight of mortals in the shape of a dove.

Semiramis was supposed to have been an incarnation of Párvaté, consort of Mahá-dévá, or Nature; which goddess was called Samirama, from a circumstance (related in one of the Puránas) of her having chosen to reside in a Sami-tree, whither she had fled from the god, her husband, in a fit of jealousy.

It is from the Sami-tree that the Indians cut the Arani, a cubic piece of wood, from which they obtain fire by drawing a cord through a perforation in the centre.

According to the fable, a fire issued from Sami-rama while performing austere devotion, which spread over the whole range of mountains near her retirement. This fire she confined to the Samif-tree, in pity to the neighboring people.

The Arani is still called by the Indians the "daughter of the Sami-tree, and mother of fire."

See an extract from the Hindoo sacred books, contained in the "Asiatic Researches."

Page 148, Last Verse, Last Two Lines.

Phrah: the original name, the Euphrates, is thought by Josephus to signify flower, or dispersion.

Page 149, First Verse.

> "*Divine Mylitta, child of light, and that*
> *Which from dark nothing formed the teeming earth.*"

The earnest and apparently pure adoration of Neantes for this goddess may proceed from some glimpses of Oriental and Grecian cosmogony caught from the scribe, his former master. One of the Venuses is said to have been the daughter of Cœlus and Light. This personification of the soul, or active principle of creation, by a form of perfect beauty, was an idea sublime, perhaps, as delightful, but, like every thing else of excessive refinement, was incapable of being generally understood in the manner first designed, and soon became perverted to the sanction of a pernicious licentiousness. The following is extracted from Enfield's "Compendium of Brucker:"—

"There were different opinions among the ancients concerning the first cause of nature. Some might possibly ascribe the origin of all things to a generating force, destitute of thought, which they conceived to be inherent in matter, without looking to any higher principle. But it is probable that the general opinion among them was that which had prevailed among the Egyptians and in the

East, and was communicated by traditions to the Greeks, — that matter or chaos existed eternally with God; that, by the divine energy of emanation, material forms went forth from him, and the visible world arose into existence. This principle being admitted, a satisfactory explanation may be given of most of the Grecian fables. Upon this supposition, their doctrines of the creation, divested of all allegory and fable, will be as follows: The first matter, containing the seeds of all future beings, existed from eternity with God. At length the divine energy, acting upon matter, produced a motion among its parts, by which those of the same kind were brought together, and those of a different kind separated, and by which, according to certain wise laws, the various forms of the material world were produced. The same energy of emanation gave existence to animals and men, *and to gods who inhabit the heavenly bodies* and various other parts of nature. Among men, those who possess a larger portion of the divine nature than others are hereby impelled to great and beneficent actions, and afford illustrious proofs of their divine original, *on account of which they are, after death, raised to a place among the gods*, and so become objects of religious worship." This is perfectly in accordance with the Christian belief, that the places left vacant by the fallen angels are to be supplied by human souls; and some of the fathers suppose that such secrets could only have been communicated to the heathen by means of angels.

PAGE 153, VERSE 3.

"*A fairer scene warm Syria never shall*
Behold."

Of the festivals given in honor of Mylitta, Herodotus has given an account; and a very full and amusing one is to be found in "Les Voyages d'Antenor." No blood flowed upon the altars of this goddess: roses, apple-blossoms, fruits, incense, and perfumes were thought more acceptable offerings. Mylitta is but one of the names of Venus.

PAGE 154, VERSE 3, LINE 1.

This might have been of the pomegranate-flower, the bright scarlet of which is very becoming to a dark complexion: it, however, respires but a faint odor. There is also a species of mimosa, which produces a splendid scarlet flower, much esteemed by the women of those climates where it is found.

PAGE 158, VERSE 1, LAST LINE.

"The gems of all Ophir."

Ophir, or Aurea Chersonesus. This pronunciation of the word is agreeable to the accent of all modern Oriental languages, which, as they are generally founded on the Hebraic, are, of course, more conformable to the ancient sweetness of a language supposed to have been that of angels and spirits than those harsh sounds to which it is now perverted by English and North-American theologists. The present Spanish pronunciation of scriptural names is very soft and delightful.

The language in which the Koran is written, and which is universally studied and spoken by learned Mahometans, is said to be a dialect of the Hebrew. The guttural sounds of the modern Castilian have probably been remotely derived from the same source.

PAGE 158, LAST VERSE, LINE 1.

"Holy Euphrates lowly murmuring swept."

Rivers were, in general, held sacred by the nations of antiquity; and to wash the hands, spit, or throw any thing of an impure nature, into the Euphrates, was punished by the Babylonians as an act of the greatest impiety. Peleus vowed to make an offering of the hair of Achilles to the stream Sperchius in case he returned victor from Troy.

PAGE 159, LAST VERSE, LINE 1.

"*Zameïa, paler than the ivory white*
That formed the pillars of her couch."

Ivory, it is said, was not much heard of till the reign of Solomon, who caused it to be brought from India to Palestine, where it was considered more precious than gold; but afterwards ivory beds and ivory palaces are frequently mentioned. The beautiful statue carved by Pygmalion of Cyprus is said to have been of ivory. Marble, however, when white and pure, was, it appears, also called ivory.

PAGE 162, LAST VERSE.

"*'Twas written on papyrus of the Nile,*
Fragrant with rose; as opening lotos white;
And gold and silver dust in sprinkles o'er it smile."

This might have been. The Greeks, however, at a later period, wrote their letters on thin smooth tablets of wood, neatly covered with wax: these were wrapped in linen, and sealed with the wax of Asia.

According to Sir William Jones and others, the manuscripts of the modern Persians are sprinkled with dust of gold and silver. These, as well as those of the Arabians, are so very beautiful, that those accustomed to them dislike to look on printed copies.

As there are many lovers of poetry who are not profound scholars, the following extract from an entertaining work may not be unacceptable:—

"Les tablettes des Grecs étaient des tables de bois, et enduites de cire: on y écrivait avec un petit stylet de cuivre, de fer, ou d'or, pointu d'un côté et plat de l'autre; ce dernier bout servait à effacer. Les Grecs portaient à la ceinture un étui nommé graphiarium où étaient renfermés ce stylet et ces tablettes.

"Les lettres que les particuliers s'écrivaient étaient sur des tables de bois mince, deliées, et enduites de cire, que l'on enveloppait de lin, et que l'on cachetait de craie, ou de cire d'Asie. A la tête de leurs lettres ils mettaient ces mots, 'Joie et prospérité:'

à leur fin, cette autre formule, 'Portez-vous bien, soyez heureux.' Les Athéniens mettaient, après leurs noms, dans leur signature, celui de leurs pères, et les pays de leur naissance; par exemple, 'Demosthène de Peanée, fils de Demosthène.'"—*Voyages d'Antenor.*

Page 164, Verse 3.

"*But as the date-tree sees her blossoms die.*"

The palm-tree is said, by a learned writer, to be "the most curious and interesting subject which the science of natural history involves." However that may be, the most eminent naturalists, ancient and modern, have apparently taken pleasure in describing it. A very full and satisfactory account of this surprising vegetable is to be found in the 'Amœnitates Exoticæ' of Kaempfer.

Page 166, Verse 3.

"*Not the string*
Of Meles' sandal, scarf about his waist,
Or feather for his arrows, was a thing
More wholly his than she."

The old Neantes appears to suppose this destructive passion to be no fault of his mistress, but thinks her inspired with it by their goddess as a punishment for former neglect. Racine, in his tragedy of "Phèdre," extenuates the crimes of that queen by a similar supposition.

NOTES TO CANTO SIXTH.

BRIDAL OF HELON.

Page 172, Verse 1.

"The bard has sung, God never formed a soul
Without its own peculiar mate."

The gods (says Plato in his "Banquet") formed man, at first, of a round figure, with two bodies and two sexes. The variety of his powers rendered him so audacious, that he made war against his creators. Jupiter was about to destroy him; but, reflecting that with him the whole human race must perish, the god contented himself with merely reducing his strength. The androgyne was accordingly separated in two parts, and Apollo received the order of perfecting them. From that time, each part, though become a separate being, seeks, desires, and feels a continual impulse, to meet the other. —*See Voyages d'Antenor*, tome i. chap. 22.

Some of the Jewish rabbins have entertained a similar opinion. According to their accounts, Adam was created male and female,—man on one side, woman on the other; and God afterwards separated the two forms that were before united.

"Les androgynes avait deux sexes, deux têtes, quatre bras, quatre pieds." — *Voyages d'Antenor.* — *See Note* to vol. I.

It was evidently from such opinions, as well as his own feelings, that Dr. Watts conceived the idea of that popular little poem which he has called "The Indian Philosopher."

The different accounts of creation are sufficiently amusing. It is said, in the Talmud, that God did not wish to create woman, because he foresaw that her husband would very soon have to complain of her perversity: he therefore waited till Adam asked her of him, and then took every precaution to make her as good as possible. He would not take her from the head, lest she should have sufficient wit and spirit to become a coquette; nor from the eyes, lest she should cast mischievous glances; nor from the mouth, lest she should listen at doors; nor from the heart, lest she should be jealous; nor from the hands or the feet, lest she should be a thief or a runaway. But every precaution was vain: she had all these defects, although drawn from the most quiet and honest part that could possibly be found about Adam. (This is merely translated from M. de Lentier.)

Page 173, Verse 1.

"And formed in every fibre for such love
As Heaven not yet had given her to share."

Souls, according to Plato, are rays of the divinity, which, ere they are shut up in the gross envelope of mortality, pass through a state of existence, during which an invincible attraction unites them two by two, and inflames them with a love pure and celestial. When embodied upon earth, these souls, thus previously united, continually seek and feel a propensity for each other, and, unless they are so happy as to meet, can never be animated by a true and genuine affection.

Page 187, Last Verse.

"He said, all o'er to radiant beauty warming:
While they, in doubt of what they looked upon,
Beheld a form dissolving, dazzling, charming;
But, ere their lips found utterance, it was gone."

Flesh is said to be composed of carbon, oxygen, hydrogen, and nitrogen. If men have already been able to discover its materials, the power of making and dissolving it at pleasure may, without inconsistency, be ascribed to beings so much superior to them as angels have ever been thought. Indeed, the supposition of such a power is the only thing that can give the least semblance of possibility to what has been related of good and evil angels.

The following passage, extracted by Brucker from the writings of Bonaventura, looks as reasonable as any thing which has ever yet been said concerning the mysterious union of spirit and body: "The formal principles of bodies are celestial bodies, which, by their accession or recession, cause the production or corruption of the inferior. It may, therefore, be concluded that there is in these occult forms a capacity of being restored to higher principles, — namely, celestial bodies; or to powers still higher than these, — that is, to separate intellectual substances, which, in their respective operations, leave traces of themselves."

PAGE 189, LAST VERSE.

"Hope, Zophiël! hope, hope, hope! thou hast a friend!"

As Zophiël appears to have no evil propensity, and commits only such crimes as are occasioned by the violence of his love, Raphaël may think it possible to induce him to repent, and ultimately obtain pardon. Haruth and Maruth were condemned for a time to inhabit a cavern beneath the Tower of Babel, with the permission of returning to heaven after a proper expiation of their offences. Their appearance in this cavern is beautifully represented in "Thalaba." These angels, according to the story, had obtained, while in heaven, such a reputation for wisdom, that they were sent on earth to judge the whole race of men. They soon, however, became so enamoured of the beautiful Zohara, that she obtained from them *the most holy of secrets.*

THE notes of "Zophiël" were written, some in Cuba, some in Canada, some at Hanover, U. S., some at Paris; and the last at Keswick, Eng., under the kind encouragement of Robert Southey, Esq., and near a window which overlooks the beautiful Lake Derwent, and the finest groups of those mountains which encircle completely that charming valley where the Greta winds over its bed of clean pebbles, looking as clear as dew.

MARIA GOWEN BROOKS.

APRIL 15, 1831.

www.ingramcontent.com/pod-product-compliance
Lightning Source LLC
LaVergne TN
LVHW020223110826
845151LV00003B/809

9781425532307